Selected Burns for Young Readers

Selected Burns for Young Readers

© 1996 Geddes & Grosset Ltd, David Dale House,
New Lanark ML11 9DJ

ISBN 1 85534 129 8

4 6 8 10 9 7 5 3

Printed and bound in the UK

Contents

Sketch of Burns, based on the portrait by Alexander Nasmyth (1758–1840), who became a friend of Burns and shared his love of Scottish landscapes.

Alloway and Mount Oliphant

Robert Burns was born on 25 January 1759 in a two-roomed thatched cottage in the village of Alloway, about two miles from the town of Ayr. The cottage, the 'auld cley biggin' as Burns later described it, was built by his father with his own hands and it survives to this day, as a national shrine to a man who is not only one of Scotland's greatest poets but who, more than any other, is also her best loved famous figure.

Burns' ancestors came from Kincardineshire where his grandfather, Robert Burnes, was a gardener in the service of the Earl Marischal. (The two-syllable 'Burnes' or 'Burness' was the family name in Kincardineshire. After their father's death, Robert Burns and his brother Gilbert adopted the usual form of the name in Ayrshire, pronounced with one syllable).

The Earl Marischal was involved in the 1715 Jacobite rebellion. The Jacobites were supporters of James II, the exiled king of England, Scotland and Ireland, who had been unwilling to swear the anti-Catholic oath imposed by an act called the Test Act which required everyone to believe in the Protestant faith. In 1715, an attempt was made to put James II's son James Francis Edward Stuart, the 'Old Pretender', on the throne. This was unsuccessful, as was the effort to bring his son Charles Edward Stuart, the 'Young Pretender' (also known as 'Bonnie Prince Charlie') to the throne in 1745. Burns liked to think that his grandfather fought for the 'Old Pretender'. There is no evidence that he did but he certainly suffered for the cause when the Earl was forced to flee to the Continent and Robert Burnes lost his job. His grandson, Robert Burns the poet, had sympathy for the Jacobite cause. This is clear from his writings and from two of his most famous songs, 'Charlie, he's my Darling' and 'It was a' for our Rightfu' King' (*see* pages 165–166).

Robert's father, William Burnes, inherited the family skill in gardening and went to Edinburgh to seek his fortune. For a time he did well, helping to landscape an area south of the city now known as The Meadows. Unfortunately work became scarce, so he moved to Ayrshire. He worked for several employers as a gardener and later rented a smallholding (the name for a very small farm) of seven and a half acres at Alloway. He needed more money and had ambitions to become a market gardener. On this land he built the clay and thatch cottage in which Robert Burns was born. It was a typical small Ayrshire farmhouse. It was a single building, long and low, with two small rooms for the humans who lived there and a stable, byre and barn that could be entered from the living rooms or from the road outside for any animal occupants. Although the house was cramped and dark it did have glazed windows and a fireplace built into the gable end of the building. These were features that many farmers could not afford.

In 1757, William Burnes married Agnes Broun, an Ayrshire farmer's daughter who was ten years younger than him. It is said that they met during the previous year at the annual fair in Maybole where Agnes lived with her grandmother. She had her first child, Robert, in 1759 and his brother, Gilbert, in 1760. They were to become the eldest of a family of seven children—four boys and three girls.

The Burnes family outside the cottage at Alloway

At the time of Robert's birth, William Burnes was thirty-eight and is described as being a 'thin, sinewy figure, about five feet eight or nine inches in height, somewhat bent with toil, his haffet locks (the hair on the sides of his head) thin and bare, with a dark swarthy complexion'. He was a well-respected man who was independent, with individuality, deep religious beliefs and a great respect for learning.

Religion played an important part in the life of the Burnes family. William Burnes was a religious man but he was not narrow-minded or severe in his outlook on life or with his children. He wrote a *Manual of Religious Belief* for his children and showed them by his own words and actions how to live sensibly and act reasonably. As Robert Burns was to write in a letter to Dr John Moore on 2 August 1787, 'I was born a very poor man's son . . . My father was gardiner to a worthy gentleman of small estate in the neighbourhood of Ayr. Had my father continued in that station, I must have marched off to be one of the little underlings about a farmhouse; but it was his dearest wish and prayer to have it in his power to keep his children under his own eye till they could discern between good and evil.' This letter can be found in the British Museum and is quoted throughout this introduction.

In 1765, Robert and Gilbert were sent to school at Alloway Mill, but the teacher left soon afterwards to become master of the Ayr workhouse (there were workhouses all over Britain, in which the poor and homeless did unpaid work in return for food and somewhere to stay). For a time, Burnes himself taught the two boys the basics of reading and writing, but he soon persuaded some of his neighbours to share with him the cost of hiring a teacher from Ayr. This was John Murdoch who was then eighteen years old and had just completed his education in Edinburgh. Murdoch was a strict teacher, and in the two and a half years he remained at Alloway, he taught Robert and Gilbert English literature and about the Old and New

Testaments. Murdoch was quick to appreciate William Burnes' early attempts to train his boys' minds. 'This had a very good effect on the boys,' he commented, 'who began to talk and reason like men much sooner than their neighbours.'

In a letter, Robert describes himself at the age of five or six: 'I was by no means a favourite with any body. I was a good deal noted for a retentive memory, a stubborn, sturdy something in my disposition.' Murdoch's own opinion of the Burns brothers is an interesting one. He wrote to Burns' biographer, Dr James Currie, after Burns' death describing the young Robert as being moody and withdrawn while Gilbert was the more outgoing brother. Robert and his younger brother Gilbert were always top of the class (except in music), although John Murdoch noted that it seemed that Gilbert had the more lively imagination and wit of the two.

Robert resembled his father, if not in appearance, then in character—honest, intelligent, hard-working, proudly independent but with a natural kindness and warmth of spirit. His father's guidance was critical to his development, particularly after John Murdoch gave up his teaching post. From the age of nine, Robert and Gilbert had little formal schooling, but their education was carried on steadily by their father, not only the three Rs but with lessons in geography and ancient and natural history.

His father's influence on his education is important, but his inspiration to be a poet was surely inherited from his mother. Agnes Broun was the eldest of six children. When her mother died, Agnes was only ten, and for two years she looked af-

ter the family until her father remarried. She was sent to
Maybole to live with her grandmother who was celebrated
locally for her knowledge of many old Scots songs and ballads.

Agnes Broun's youngest daughter, Isabella (later Mrs
Begg), said of her mother, 'She was rather under the average height; inclined to plumpness, but neat, shapely, and
full of energy; having a beautiful pink-and-white complexion,
a fine square forehead, pale red hair, but dark eyebrows,
and dark eyes often ablaze with a temper difficult to con-
trol. Her disposition was naturally cheerful; her manner,
easy and collected; her address, simple and unpresuming;
and her judgement uncommonly sound and good.'

Although she could not read, Agnes Broun was a lively
and intelligent woman who knew many traditional poems
and tales. The old songs meant a great deal to her; she pos-
sessed a fine musical ear and loved singing. The little cottage at Alloway echoed with her lilting voice and there can
be little doubt where Robert acquired his interest in Scots
folksong.

Robert took his temperament, his poetic talent and his
imagination chiefly from his mother, but another important influence in his early years was old Betty Davidson.
She was distantly related to Agnes Broun and used to help
about the house and byre, staying with the family for long
periods. Robert wrote that 'she had, I suppose, the largest
collection in the country of tales and songs concerning
devils, ghosts, fairies, brownies, witches, warlocks, spun-
kies, kelpies, elf-candles, dead-lights, wraiths, apparitions,

cantraips, giants, enchanted towers, dragons and other trumpery.' Her tales had a strong effect on the young Burns' imagination, and as well as possibly causing him nightmares, such tales were to influence Robert Burns' greatest long poem, *Tam o' Shanter* (*see* page 140).

Towards the end of 1765, William Burnes decided the time had come to move on. Two daughters, Agnes and Annabella, had been born and the cottage at Alloway was now much too small for the growing family. Also, Burnes knew that when his two boys were nine or so they would have to be hired out to work on some neighbouring farm. Burnes was determined to keep his family together, and he asked his employer, Provost Fergusson, for the lease of a vacant seventy-acre moorland farm at Mount Oliphant which he owned. Fergusson agreed, and when Burnes had difficulty in disposing of the land and cottage at Alloway, Fergusson offered to lend his new tenant enough money to stock the farm. It was a loan Burnes was to regret, because accepting Fergusson's apparently generous gesture turned out to be a very bad move.

Gilbert Burns recalled that the farm at Mount Oliphant was 'almost the very poorest soil I know in a state of cultivation'. It was a grim existence on the farm. The extra room that the family so badly needed turned out to be an attic where the two boys had to sleep. Gilbert and Robert had no boys of their own age to mix with, indeed they rarely saw anyone but the members of their own family. Their father still thought that their education was important and tried to increase their knowledge and powers of reasoning by discussing subjects with them as if they were adults.

Food was very meagre and their work was exhausting. At the age of thirteen, Robert had to assist in the threshing of the corn by hand (beating stalks of corn to separate the grain from the husks and straw), and at the age of fifteen he was the main labourer on the farm.

But the family stayed and struggled; more children were born—William in 1767, John in 1769 and Isabella in 1771—Robert and Gilbert were growing up, and their father continued his constant fight to maintain and improve his family's wellbeing. The need for their help on the farm meant that Robert and Gilbert made the trip to Alloway to attend Murdoch's school less frequently. Then, in 1768, Murdoch moved to another and better-paid teaching post in Carrick and the link with the Burnes family was temporarily broken.

The books most commonly used at Murdoch's school were the Bible, a spelling book, Fisher's English Grammar and, most significantly for Robert, *Masson's Collection of Prose and Verse*, an anthology of the major English poets— Shakespeare, Milton, Dryden, Gray—and selections of eighteenth-century writing. Robert had his early favourites. 'The two first books I ever read in private, and which gave me more pleasure than any two books I ever read again, were *The Life of Hannibal,* and *The History of Sir William Wallace*. Hannibal gave my young ideas such a turn that I used to strut in raptures up and down after the recruiting drum and bagpipe, and wish myself tall enough to be a soldier; while the story of Wallace poured a Scottish prejudice in my veins which will boil along there till the floodgates of life shut in eternal rest.'

There were always books in the house at Mount Oliphant, from neighbours and friends or bought from travelling salesmen; William Burnes even subscribed to a book society in Ayr. The reading matter was all fairly hard going, and, to relieve it, a relative was despatched to Ayr to buy a book to teach letter-writing. Fortunately for Robert, a small collection of letters by eminent writers was bought by mistake. This book inspired Robert with a strong desire to excel in letter-writing and gave him examples by some of the finest writers in the language.

In 1772, Robert and Gilbert were sent for the summer to a school in Dalrymple to improve their handwriting. They attended week about because they could not both be spared from the farm at the same time. Education was not free in those days and William Burnes could also not afford to pay two lots of school fees. When John Murdoch returned to teach at the Ayr burgh school, Robert was sent to stay with the teacher—literally to share his bed—so the two of them were together virtually twenty-four hours a day. For three weeks during the summer of 1773, Robert revised his English grammar and studied French and Latin. He took a French dictionary and a book of French grammar back to the farm and it seems likely that he continued his studies on his own for he later showed ability in the language. But he made little progress with Latin.

All the while, as a poor farmer's son, he had to work hard and suffer loneliness and continuous exhaustion. No doubt the time he spent at school, where at least he would have met other boys of his own age, was a blessed relief. 'I was a dexterous ploughman for my age,' says the poet, and his body, used to daily toil and continually exposed to every kind of weather, looked robust and strong beyond his years.

Before he was sixteen years old, Robert had worked his way through a large and very varied amount of literature. John Murdoch's teaching and Robert's own aptitude had made him an excellent English scholar. Wherever he went he carried with him a book of songs. 'I pored over them, driving my cart or walking to labour, song by song, verse by verse, carefully noting the true, tender or sublime from affectation and fustian.'

At the age of fifteen, Robert Burns 'committed the sin of Rhyme'—he fell in love and wrote his first song, 'Handsome Nell' (*see* page 191):

> O once I lov'd a bonnie lass,
>> An aye I love her still,
> An' whilst that virtue warms my breast
>> I'll love my handsome Nell.

'You know your country custom of coupling a man and woman together as partners in the labours of Harvest,' Robert wrote. 'In my fifteenth autumn my partner was a bewitching creature who just counted an autumn less. My scarcity of English denies me the power of doing her jus-

tice in that language, but you know the Scotch idiom. She
was a bonnie, sweet sonsie lass. In short, she altogether unwittingly to herself, initiated me in a certain delicious Passion, which in spite of acid Disappointment, gin-horse
Prudence, and bookworm Philosophy, I hold to be the first
of human joys, our dearest pleasure here below. . . . I did
not know well myself, why I liked so much to loiter behind with her, when returning in the evening from our labours; why the tones of her voice made my heartstrings
thrill like an Eolian harp; and particularly, why my pulse
beat such a furious ratann when I looked and fingered over
her hand, to pick out the nettle-stings and thistles. . . .
Thus with me began Love and Poesy.'

Robert's affair with Nelly Kilpatrick was an innocent
one, as too most probably was his encounter with Peggy
Thompson, when at the age of seventeen he was sent to a

'My pulse beat a furious ratann when I looked over her hand.'

school at Kirkoswald for the summer. Kirkoswald was inland from the Ayrshire coast, renowned for smuggling.

'The contraband trade [illegally imported or exported
goods] was at that time very successful; scenes of swaggering riot and roaring dissipation were as yet new to me; and
I was no enemy to social life,' Robert writes. 'Here, though
I learned to look unconcernedly on a large tavern-bill, and
mix without fear in a drunken squabble, yet I went on with
a high hand in my Geometry; till the sun entered Virgo, a
month which is always a carnival in my bosom, a charming
Fillette who lived next door to the school overset my Trigo-
nometry, and set me off at a tangent from the sphere of my
studies. . . . Stepping out to the garden one charming noon,
to take the sun's altitude, I met with my Angel. . . . It was vain
to think of doing any more good at school. . . . I did nothing
but craze the faculties of my soul about her, or steal out to
meet with her. . . .'

Peggy Thompson, the 'charming Fillette', remained dear
to Robert. Later he presented her with an inscribed copy
of the Kilmarnock poems.

Almost all Burns' early poems have love as their theme.
Later he was to write, 'If anything on earth deserves the
name of rapture or transport it is the feelings of green
eighteen in the company of the mistress of his heart when
she repays him with an equal return of affection. For my
own part I never had the least thought or inclination of
turning Poet till I got once heartily in Love, and then
Rhyme and Song were, in a manner, the spontaneous language of my heart.'

In November 1769, Burnes' landlord died and the factor
of the estate, whose job it was to bring in arrears of rent,
proved less sympathetic than Fergusson to Burnes' inability
to pay his dues on time. The old man's health was failing
and the land at Mount Oliphant continued to be unpro-
ductive. As a way out of his troubles, Burnes abandoned
Mount Oliphant as soon as his lease expired, and with the
debt to Fergusson's heirs carried over to the new enter-
prise, he took the lease of a farm at Lochlea which lay a
few miles further inland in more fertile country. There was
no written agreement with his new landlord, an Ayr mer-
chant named David McClure. The bargain was sealed on a
handshake, which was a very common way of doing business in those times. The absence of any formal agreement
was to bring about Burnes' ruin in costly litigation (a legal
procedure to prove one's claim to something) and was a
major factor in causing his death. But, in 1777, when
William and Agnes Burnes and their seven children moved
to Lochlea, they were full of hope for the future. Robert
was then nineteen, he was well read and could rhyme and
was constantly in love with some 'fair enslaver'.

Lochlea and Mossgiel

THE farm at Lochlea could be reached down a track that branched off midway along the road between Tarbolton and Mauchline. Although it was some four hundred feet above sea level, Lochlea was less bleak than Mount Oliphant, but the land was swampy and undrained. William Burnes paid a high rent and the bargain he struck turned out to be a poor one.

Nevertheless, the Burnes family managed to survive for four years. They worked hard together and Robert came to think of this time as one of the happiest and most settled periods of his life. He read constantly and more widely than before. Indeed, William Burnes saw to it that all his children were suitably occupied when they were not working in the fields—or sleeping. You can imagine the family assembled around the table at meal times, each with a spoon in one hand and a book in the other.

Robert made new friends and found new interests in Tarbolton, the larger of the nearby towns. He attended a dancing school to improve his social graces. He described himself as 'the most ungainly, awkward boy in the parish'. He even persuaded his father, who at first objected to so frivolous a pastime, to allow other members of the family to attend.

'Each with a spoon in one hand and a book in the other'

His closest friend was David Sillar, a farmer's son, minor poet and fiddle player. Others included a neighbouring farmer, John Rankine, the local exciseman (tax collector), James Findlay, and a group of young men who were his fellow founder members of the Bachelors' Club. This club, which may have been Robert's idea—certainly he was one of its leading figures—existed to debate various topics. The rules of the club laid down that 'Every man proper for a member of this Society, must have a frank, honest, open heart; above anything dirty or mean; and must be a professed lover of one or more of the female sex.' The club met in a building in Tarbolton, which now serves as a Burns museum.

Many of Burns' poems show his flirtatious nature with women, which is clear in a poem like 'The Tarbolton Lasses'. But Robert was not always successful in love. 'As in every other warfare in this world,' he said, 'my fortune was various; sometimes I was received with favour, and sometimes I was mortified with a repulse.'

One who did apparently reject him was Alison (Ellison) Begbie, a servant girl from a neighbouring farm. Robert addressed at least five letters to her in the course of his courtship, although the originals have never been traced. In the fourth of these he proposes marriage. 'There is one thing, my dear, which I earnestly request of you, and it is this: that you would soon either put an end to my hopes by a peremptory refusal, or cure me of my fears by a generous consent.' Alison Begbie was probably the inspiration for three poems, the loveliest of which is 'Mary Morison' (*see* page 193).

On 4 July 1781, Robert became a Freemason. The Freemasons are a secret society with only male members whose main aim is to help each other with their careers. The organisation is still widespread today. This was an important step in his career. The influential friends he acquired as fellow masons were to be the greatest help to him in his future years. Robert made rapid progress, becoming Depute Master of his Lodge. He often spoke of one of his proudest moments, the famous toast to him at St Andrew's Lodge, Edinburgh, by the Grand Master, 'Caledonia, and Caledonia's Bard, brother Burns . . . which rung through the whole Assembly with multiplied honours and repeated acclamations.'

Also in the summer of 1781, he began a project which was to Robert, at the age of twenty two, away from the drudgery of farm labouring and the cosy circle of his family. Part of the land at Lochlea had been given over to flax growing, a plant which is grown for its seeds and for the fibres of its stems which can be made into linen fabrics. The crop could be made more profitable if the grower was able to prepare, or 'heckle', the flax for the spinners. So Robert moved to Irvine, then the main centre for flax dressing and a busy seaport even larger than Ayr, to learn the trade. He stayed in a house in a district known as Glasgow Vennel with a man named Peacock who may have been related to his mother. His period as a 'heckler' was not a success. The shop in which he worked with a partner was burned down during the New Year celebrations in 1782. 'It was,' he says, 'an unlucky affair. As we were giving a welcome carousal to the New Year, the shop took fire and burned to ashes; and I was left, like a true poet, without a sixpence.'

More important than the flax-dressing experiment to Robert was his meeting with Richard Brown, a young seaman widely experienced in the ways of the world. He was a man of some ability, for later he became the master of a large West Indiaman (a ship which is used in making trade with India) based on the Thames in London. He and Robert were to become firm friends and it is clear from Robert's autobiographical letter that Brown was a great influence on the two main streams of his life— poetry and his love of women. Brown was fond of poetry and Robert, in one of his letters, recalls a Sunday spent in Eglinton Woods just outside the town when he repeated some of his poems to the seaman. Brown urged Robert to send his verses to a magazine. 'Twas actually this that gave me an idea of my own pieces which encouraged me to endeavour at the character of a Poet.'

Robert enjoyed the full and free life in Irvine and lingered in the town, but by March 1782 he had to return to the farm at Lochlea. His father's health was failing and the dispute with landlord McClure over payment for improvements to the farm was worrying William Burnes into his grave. To settle the dispute Burnes took his case to the Court of Session in Edinburgh. In January 1784, a decision was eventually made in Burnes' favour, but the case had exhausted both his savings and his strength.

William Burnes died on 13 February 1784. Many people admired his good character. John Murdoch said of him that 'he was a tender and affectionate father who took pleasure in leading his children in the path of virtue.' His son Robert immortalised William as 'the saint, the father, and the hus-

'He took pleasure in leading his children in the path of virtue.'

band' of *The Cotter's Saturday Night* (*see* page 127). 'I have met few,' he said, 'who understood men, their manners, and their ways, equal to my father.' Burnes was buried in the Auld Kirkyard at Alloway, half a mile from the cottage he built for Agnes Broun, and his tombstone bears a final epitaph written by his son.

Robert Burns was now head of the family and was responsible for providing for them. He found a good friend in a fellow mason, a Mauchline lawyer named Gavin Hamilton. He advised the Burnes children to claim back wages for their work as labourers on the farm against their father's estate. This gave them prior claim over other creditors and enough money to enable Robert and Gilbert to lease the farm of Mossgiel some two miles to the southeast of Lochlea.

All the family's money was invested in the Mossgiel farm, and for four years they had to work very hard to make a living. During the whole of this time, the brothers allowed themselves each only £7 a year in wages. The position of the farm and the soil surrounding it were not ideal, but Nature alone could not be blamed for the Burns' lack of success as farmers. Robert was determined to take his responsibilities seriously. He devoted himself to the business of running the farm efficiently. 'I read farming books; I calculated crops; I attended markets . . . but the first year from unfortunately buying in bad seed, the second from a late harvest, we lost half of both our crops.'

Robert was now twenty-five. For ten years, when he had had some time to himself away from his duties at the farm, he had read wisely and widely. He had been an impressive speaker in the debates of the Tarbolton Bachelors' Club; he had shed much of his natural shyness at masonic gatherings and village dances; he had shown himself to be a worthy opponent when it came to skilled argument. From early manhood he was what you might call an idealist, someone who sees or imagines the best of a person or situation when this may not actually be true. This idealism paired with a certain fickleness in his relationships with women, meant that he had many romances, which were frequently short-lived, and in which he often treated women rather badly.

One of his romances was with Elizabeth Paton, a servant at Lochlea during the unhappy days when William Burnes lay dying with consumption (this is now more commonly known as tuberculosis or TB). Elizabeth was said to be rather plain but with a good figure. She probably fitted brother Gilbert's acute assessment of Robert's 'fair charmers', who were 'instantly invested with a sufficient stock of charms, out of the plentiful stores of his own imagination.' Robert's talent for romantic poetry perhaps also gave him this tendency to idealise his loves.

Elizabeth Paton is remembered as the mother of Robert's first child. On 22 May 1785, she gave birth to a daughter, Elizabeth, whom Robert acknowledged as his. There may have been talk of marriage, but the family as a whole would certainly have opposed it and such affairs were not uncommon in rural life at that time. When Burns had earned some money from the first edition of his poems, he sent some money to Elizabeth for the upkeep of her child. It is often said of Burns that he showed more affection for the children of his loves than he did for their mothers.

As a poet, Robert's local renown was based not on his songs, which were for private reading, but on his more political poems, which discussed the often bigoted behaviour of the Kirk, the Scottish word for church, and on his humorous and often very insulting satires on certain well-known Ayrshire folk. A work is a satire when it ridicules a topical issue or a well-known person in an ironic, and often humorous way, and Burns was a master of this. An example of such a satire is 'The Twa Herds' (not included in this book) which dared to attack the Kirk and named particular Scottish ministers of the day. It was followed by another satire, 'Holy Willie's Prayer' (see page 155), which portrayed a character whose public image as a religious man was not matched by his real personality. Despite these attacks, Burns was essentially a religious and kindly man. Those who admired his early satires were the more unorthodox and freethinking of his countrymen and they included many of his closest friends.

Robert first met his future wife, Jean Armour, sometime in 1784. She was one of the 'Mauchline Belles', the daughter of a master mason in the village. She knew Burns' reputation for short-lived romances and was not frightened by it, going out of her way to make his acquaintance. They fell genuinely in love. Jean became pregnant in February 1786. Robert intended to marry her and may have made a written declaration to this effect which by Scots law was a formal contract. It is said that Jean's father, who was outraged by the affair, destroyed the document and forced Jean to separate from Burns. The Armours had no wish to acquire a penniless son-in-law and Jean was packed off to stay with relatives in Paisley. Robert was deeply hurt by what he considered Jean's betrayal.

Robert decided that he would emigrate to the West Indies. He intended to try his fortune in Jamaica where many of his countrymen were plantation managers. Another reason for wanting to escape was his mysterious affair with Mary Campbell which ended in tragedy. Almost immediately after his argument with the Armour family the poet plighted his troth to Mary (he made a vow of betrothal that in those days was seen to be as important as a marriage vow—this was often done by a simple making of vows and an exchange of Bibles). He had put himself in the awkward position of having promised marriage to two girls at the same time. He suggested that Mary might accompany him to the West Indies. She left her parents' home in Campbeltown and went to Greenock. Very soon afterwards she died. The cause of her death is unknown, although the most popular view is that she died in childbirth, to be forgotten for the moment by Burns but to live forever in memory as his 'Highland Mary' (*see* page 206). The verses she inspired Burns to write are not considered by critics to be his best work. It is the romantic notion of her as the 'ideal maiden' created by early biographers that has survived so long.

From the way Burns spoke of her several years after the episode, it seems that his memory of her, and probably his guilt over her death, remained strong in his conscience.

A post had been secured for Burns in Jamaica, but he could not afford to pay for his passage. The time of his departure coincided with the publication of his first volume of poems at Kilmarnock in July 1786. One of his motives for publishing was probably to raise money to pay for his West Indian trip. But a series of events made him change his mind. First, the death of Mary Campbell meant he could no longer be accused of bigamy. Second, Jean Armour was near her the end of her pregnancy, and when she gave birth to twins, Robert was overjoyed . . . 'Armour has just brought me a fine boy and girl at one throw. God bless the little dears!' Third, and most important, the Kilmarnock edition of his poems was a great success and made him more famous than he had ever expected.

The book contained many of Burns' most celebrated poems, among them 'The Twa Dogs' (*see* page 67), 'The Jolly Beggars' (*see* page 77), 'The Author's Earnest Cry and Prayer' (*see* page 97), 'The Cotter's Saturday Night' (*see* page 127), 'To a Mouse' (*see* page 105) and 'To a Mountain Daisy' (*see* page 113) as well as some of his most popular songs.

'I was at that time resident in Galloway,' wrote Robert Heron, Burns' biographer, 'and I can well remember how even ploughboys and maidservants would have gladly bestowed the wages they earned the most hardly, and which they wanted to purchase necessary clothing, if they might but procure the works of Burns.'

The first edition of this collection of verses brought the author only £20 direct return, but it spread his fame much wider and introduced him to the literati (the literary and scholarly society) of Edinburgh.

Edinburgh

Burns decided to set out for the capital city in November 1786 to arrange a second edition of his work. This was encouraged by Dr Blacklock, a blind Edinburgh poet of some distinction whom Burns respected. Dr Blacklock was enthusiastic about the poems in the Kilmarnock edition, and Burns was filled with happy disbelief that such a respected man could be an admirer of his work.

Within a fortnight of his arrival in Edinburgh the poet was already mixing with important members of Edinburgh society.

Owing to his popularity in Ayrshire, Burns was fairly well accustomed to meeting important and impressive people. He was neither shy nor awkward in the company of those to whom he was introduced. He was treated as an equal, or so it seemed, by the aristocrats, university professors, ministers and advocates who became his friends and patrons. Those whom he met were charmed by his appearance and manners and his frank, vigorous but modest conversation. In particular he appealed to the ladies of fashion, led by Jane, Duchess of Gordon, who held court both in Edinburgh and London and counted among her admirers the prime minister,

William Pitt, and even the king himself. She invited Burns to several of her drawing-room parties, accompanied him to balls and assemblies and generally behaved in a way that caused a minor scandal. Burns did not let all this go to his head and behaved modestly. 'The attentions he received,' said Dugald Stewart, professor at Edinburgh University, 'from all ranks and descriptions of persons were such as would have turned any head but his own.'

Sir Walter Scott, the Scottish novelist famous for his historical novels such as *Waverley*, *The Antiquary*, *Old Mortality*, *The Heart of Midlothian* and *The Bride of Lammermoor*, was a lad of fifteen when he met Burns. He wrote a vivid description of his appearance: 'His person was strong and robust; his manners rustic, not clownish; a sort of dignified plainness and simplicity, which received part of its effect, perhaps, from one's knowledge of his extraordinary tal-

Burns recites his poems to an Edinburgh society gathering

ents. . . . I think his countenance was more massive than it looks in any of the portraits. I would have taken the poet, had I not known what he was, for a very sagacious country farmer of the old Scottish school.'

Burns was about five feet ten inches in height, with a slight stoop due to years of working at the plough. He was dark-haired, with keen black glowing eyes such as Scott declared he had never seen in any other person, ' . . . his conversation free, unaffected, ever interesting; his dress midway between the holiday costume of a farmer and that of the company with which he now associated.'

Burns soon became a popular figure in Edinburgh. He went from his society meetings, where he debated with professors and turned the heads of duchesses, to share a bed in the garret (an attic) of John Richmond, an old friend from Ayrshire who was then a lawyer's clerk in Edinburgh. The friends lodged in the house of Mrs Carfrae in Baxter's Close, Lawnmarket, where together they paid three shillings a week for the room.

Because of the cramped living conditions in the Old Town of Edinburgh, the various levels of society mixed freely with each other. The tenement buildings set in crowded closes and narrow wynds housed a great variety of types, occupations and classes. The 'better classes' lived in the middle flats, with the really poor below them at ground level and the shopkeepers and artisans above them; in the attics lived clerks and labourers; and everyone had to squeeze past each other, up and down their narrow winding stairs.

The confined quarters in which most of Edinburgh's

The teeming streets of the Old Town of Edinburgh

citizens lived forced men out into the streets for entertainment and leisure. Nightly, the taverns and eating houses were packed with the towns inhabitants. There were many drinking clubs, particularly those that attracted educated men, musicians, artists, philosophers and lawyers. Burns joined a drinking club called the Crochallan Fencibles which pretended to be a military organisation with its members holding mock military titles. Burns composed many bawdy songs for the club's members which were later published under the title *The Merry Muses of Caledonia*. These verses, full of vitality, vulgarity and humour, remained unpublished for many years until the freer atmosphere of modern times allowed their publication.

Despite being an undoubted success, Burns was still judged by his background and thought of as the 'unlettered ploughman poet', a picture that Burns lived up to when it suited him. The great men who patronised him could not have realised that his name and reputation would long outlive their own. Today the chief claim to fame of such people as Dugald Stewart and Hugh Blair is their association with Burns. Burns was fully aware of his limitations as a man and as a poet, and that being a celebrity would probably be a very short-lived experience, so he had the good sense and modesty to be uneasy with his fame.

In 1787 the second edition of the poems was published. Burns had selected the Edinburgh publisher and bookseller, William Creech, as his agent. Creech arranged the printing and binding of the book but the cost of the production of the book was entirely paid for by Burns. The Caledonian Hunt, an association of country gentlemen whose interests included field sports and social gatherings, subscribed for 100 copies of the book, which caused Burns to dedicate the first Edinburgh edition to the Hunt. Other subscribers included the Earl of Glencairn and the Marquis of Graham, and so great was the interest stimulated by Burns' aristocratic friends that all the copies of the second edition were reserved before publication. A third edition was hastily reset and published simultaneously.

Twenty-two poems and songs were added to those in the original Kilmarnock edition, including the 'Address to a Haggis' (*see* page 175), which every year is performed at Burns Suppers throughout the world, and 'Green Grow the Rashes, 0' (*see* page 194).

According to Burns, a total 3,000 copies were printed, a

large enough number for the time. Burns thought there could be little demand for further editions and agreed to Creech's suggestion that he accept an extra one hundred guineas from the publisher in return for the copyright. Burns did not receive the money for this until the spring of 1788. This prevented Burns' planned move back to farming in Dumfriesshire. He was still concerned about how to earn a living in the future. He wrote to Mrs Frances Dunlop of Dunlop House, one of his most faithful friends with whom he corresponded over a period of ten years, to discuss alternative careers. He again considered emigrating to the West Indies, and then of buying a commission in the army. Mrs Dunlop responded by suggesting that he should apply for the chair of agriculture at Edinburgh University!

In the end he decided to return to farming and the life to which he had been bred. He had been offered some land in Dumfries. He needed to inspect this land, so on his way there he made the first of his tours of Scotland. He had expressed a desire 'to make leisurely pilgrimages through Caledonia'. In any event, he could not finally leave Edinburgh until Creech paid up.

Burns spent the summer of 1787 travelling, visiting some of the classic scenes of Scottish history and romance. Until then he had seen little outside his native Ayrshire and the capital city. His first tour was to the Border country, crossing the Tweed at Coldstream where he stood on English soil for the first time. With his companion, Robert Ainslie, Burns visited such places as Roxburgh, Jedburgh, Dryburgh and Melrose, noting the scenery and admiring the

Burns toured the Border country with Robert Ainslie

ruins which he wrote up in a journal of his tour. He journeyed across northern England to Carlisle and eventually made his way to Dumfries where he was made a freeman of the town.

Burns inspected the farm at Ellisland on the Dalswinton estate in Dumfries and was not greatly impressed. On 9 June he called at Mossgiel to find things not going well with Gilbert and the family (two months later he made an interest-free loan of £180 to Gilbert, which must have been quite a sacrifice). He met again with Jean Armour. This time he had the full approval of her parents whose attitude towards Burns was totally changed now that he had found fame and success. Not surprisingly, the poet found himself incapable of settling down in the humble circles of his family life in Ayrshire.

Two weeks later he was off on his first Highland tour; perhaps Burns was still haunted by the memory of Mary Campbell. He travelled alone and left no record of his exact route although his letters reveal he visited Inveraray and Dumbarton. Returning to Mossgiel in July, he stayed awhile with Jean and composed the draft of his famous autobiographical letter to Dr Moore, quoted throughout this text.

He returned to Edinburgh in August probably to try to recover more of the money that Creech owed him. He also planned a more extensive tour of the Highlands with William Nicol, who taught at the High School in the city. This time Burns kept another journal which was later to be published. He visited Bannockburn, Killiecrankie and Culloden, to which he made brief patriotic references, ventured as far north as Elgin and Inverness, called at Aberdeen and spent some time among his relatives in the country of his ancestors around Stonehaven. Burns and his companion travelled in a chaise some 600 miles in twenty-two days.

Burns' final tour in October 1787 was along the Ochils through Linlithgow to Stirling. The principal point of interest in this journey was a stay at Harvieston House in the Devon Valley near Stirling where Burns renewed acquaintance with Margaret Chalmers, whose family lived on a farm near Mauchline and whom he had met in Edinburgh. Burns courted her for eight days, and according to Margaret herself, proposed marriage which she refused. It has been said that such a match would have given Burns the kind of woman who was his social and intellectual equal. It seems Burns thought so: 'When I think I have met with you, and have lived more of real life with you in eight days than I can do with almost anybody I meet with in eight years—when I think on the improbability of meeting you in this world again—I could sit down and cry like a child!' Margaret Chalmers married an Edinburgh banker, Lewis Hay, in December 1788, and as Burns had said, it is improbable that they met again.

Back in Edinburgh once more, Burns worked enthusiastically on the task of collecting Scottish songs with an Edinburgh engraver, James Johnson, who was compiling the first volume of *The Scots Musical Museum*. His delight in this work was overshadowed by continuing doubts about his future. Another visit to Ellisland again left him undecided about accepting the farm, and still Creech had not paid up. In Edinburgh society, as he had predicted, Burns was not the celebrity that he once had been and he knew he must leave the capital and make his living in a more everyday way. In December 1787, he attended a party given by the sister of revenue officer John Nimmo. The party was notable, not for the difference it made to his career, but because he was introduced to Mrs McLehose with whom he had a passionate but unfulfilled romance.

Agnes McLehose, Nancy to her friends, was small and pretty. She and Burns were immediately attracted to each other and neither made any attempt to conceal the fact. Married at the age of seventeen, Nancy was badly treated by her husband and left him after four and a half years. She had borne three children (one dying in infancy) and was carrying a fourth. Her husband had taken the children from her by force, then because of debt was thrown into prison. On his release he left the country, never to return, leaving Nancy to fend for herself and the children. Since 1782 Nancy had lived in Edinburgh under the protection of her cousin, William Craig.

Burns' reaction to falling in love yet again was typical: he began a lengthy romantic correspondence with Nancy in which they addressed each other by the names of Sylvander and Clarinda. Nancy was aware that in the eyes of society and in those of her cousin, on whom she depended, her position as a married woman was a delicate one. She seems to have held Burns at arm's length while continuing to inflame his passion.

Burns wrote to his friend Richard Brown, 'Almighty Love still "reigns and revels" in my bosom; and I am at this moment ready to hang myself for a young Edinburgh widow.'

Burns' affair with Nancy showed no signs of progressing, and his feelings for her beginning to cool, he rode off from Edinburgh to return to Mossgiel. Back in Ayrshire, events moved swiftly. He took up again with Jean Armour who was about to give birth to another set of twins—girls who both died within a few weeks of their birth—and in somewhat mysterious circumstances, married her. He also stopped wavering over his decision whether or not to take Ellisland Farm and signed the lease in the spring of 1788.

Through the influence of Robert Graham of Fintry, a

commissioner of the Scottish Board of Excise, the government organisation responsible for the collection of tax. Burns was granted a six-week course of instruction designed to fit him to be an exciseman and—this completed—he moved into Ellisland in June to prepare the place for Jean and his one surviving child, Robert (the other twin, Jean, had died late in 1787).

Nancy McLehose heard of Burns' marriage from his friend, Robert Ainslie, who also had a mild flirtation with Nancy. She maintained silence for a year then wrote again to Burns, who replied, not to Clarinda but to 'My dearest Nancy'. Their letters continued to flow, and they finally met and parted for the last time in December 1791. In her journal forty years later Nancy wrote on 6 December 1831: 'This day I can never forget. Parted with Burns, in the year 1791, never more to meet in this world. Oh, may we meet in Heaven.' Burns expressed his genuine love for Nancy in one of his most beautiful songs, 'Ae Fond Kiss' (*see* page 203).

Ellisland and Dumfries

WHILE a house was being built at Ellisland, Burns spent a bleak and lonely summer in the previous tenant's dwelling, which was little more than a hut, and began enclosing the farm and making other improvements. Every ten days or so he journeyed more than forty miles to visit Jean at Mauchline and left his farm workers and the builders unsupervised. The house was not ready on time, and Burns wrote despairing letters to his contractors pleading with them to finish the job quickly: 'I am distressed with the want of my house in a most provoking manner. . . . For G–d's sake let me but within the shell of it!'

Burns missed Jean's companionship ' . . . I have got the handsomest figure, the sweetest temper, the soundest constitution, and the kindest heart in the country.' However, it was not until May 1789 that he and Jean were able to move into the house. During the period of waiting he wrote numerous letters, particularly to Mrs Dunlop, who remained his most constant correspondent. By this time Burns was thoroughly disillusioned by the prospect of running the farm at Ellisland, as he revealed in a letter to his friend Robert Graham, on whom he was depending to help him get a job with the Excise: 'My farm, now that I have tried

Burns consoled himself by writing numerous letters

it a little, tho' I think it will in time be a saving bargain, yet
does by no means promise to be such a Pennyworth as I
was taught to expect. It is in the last stage of worn-out
poverty, and will take some time before it pays the rent. I
might have had the cash to supply the deficiencies of these
hungry years, but I have a younger brother and three sisters, on a farm in Ayrshire; and it took all my surplus, over
what I thought necessary for my farming capital, to save
not only the comfort but the very existence of that fireside
family-circle from impending destruction. This was done
before I took the farm; and rather than abstract my money
from my brother, a circumstance which would ruin him, I
will resign the farm and enter immediately into the service
of your Honours [the Excise Board].'

He also asked that he should be considered for the post of Excise Officer for the district, pointing out that the removal of the present holder of the post might be arranged without inconvenience as the gentleman had lately inherited a legacy and had become 'quite opulent'. Burns got his way eventually, and in September 1789 was given the district at a salary of £50 a year, a sum that compared favourably with the wage of the average minister or schoolteacher. He wrote to Mrs Dunlop: 'Five days in the week, or four at least, I must be on horseback, and very frequently ride thirty or forty miles ere I return; besides four different kinds of book-keeping to post every day.' With less time to devote to the farm, Burns directed its activities towards dairying, keeping twelve cows from which Jean produced milk, butter and cheese.

Excise work was a complicated business in the eighteenth century. Many different goods were taxed and the rates varied widely according to quality, kind and size. A list of some of the items subject to excise duty published in an article in the Burns Chronicle of 1898 begins with 'auctions, bricks and tiles, beer, candles' and ends with 'tea, tobacco, snuff, wine and wire'. An officer had to provide his own horse, pay his own expenses and keep detailed records. Although Burns enjoyed the work, and his efficiency pleased his superiors, the work was not suited to his now weakened constitution and failing health. He continued to suffer from heart trouble, was in pain from a knee injury sustained in Edinburgh and had frequent bouts of influenza. No wonder that by the end of 1789 Burns described himself as 'groaning under the miseries of a diseased nervous system'. But he battled on with his usual cheerfulness and determination.

Burns was welcomed readily by Nithsdale society, and one of the first to become his friend was the antiquarian (someone who collects or studies old objects) and amateur musician Robert Riddel of Glenriddel, an estate in Dumfriesshire. He and Burns had a common interest in Scottish song and literature. He got Burns to help form a parish library for the benefit of the tenant farmers. Burns played a full part in local community life. He wrote election ballads to help the Tory candidate; kept up an active interest in politics; defended his Liberal friends in the Ayrshire clergy; wrote prologues for special benefit performances at the Dumfries theatre; and on the hundredth anniversary of the landing in Britain of William of Orange, expressed his sympathy with the Stuart cause (i.e. the aim of the Jacobites, to return a Stuart to the Throne).

Despite the pressures of overwork and ill health, Burns seemed happy at Ellisland. He was content with his marriage to Jean whose love for Burns expressed itself in an acceptance of the man for what he was—for his failings as well as his virtues.

In November 1791, Burns finally left farming in disgust when his landlord, who wanted to sell Ellisland, disposed of it to a neighbour for £1900 and was able to release Burns from his obligations. The family moved to Dumfries where they rented part of a house in a street near the river, known then as the Stinking or Wee Vennel. From the proceeds of the sale of his crops, stock and equipment at Ellisland, Burns settled several outstanding debts. He paid for the erection of a tombstone over the grave of Robert Fergusson, the Scots poet whom Burns admired and whose influence on his own work he generously acknowledged. Burns wrote to Peter Hill who acted as banker for him in Edinburgh, ' . . . £5 10s per acct I owe to Mr Robert Burn, Architect, for erecting the stone over poor Fergusson. He has been two years on erecting it, after I commissioned him for it; and I have been two years paying him, after he sent me his account; so he and I are quits. He had the *hardiesse* [boldness] to ask me interest on the sum; but considering that the money was due by one Poet, for putting a tombstone over another, he may, with grateful surprise, thank Heaven that ever he saw a farthing of it.'

During his stay at Ellisland, Burns not only found time to write many letters, but his Muse (a word he often liked to use to describe his inspiration to write) was also active. He wrote much occasional verse—epistles, dedications and elegies, and one masterpiece, *Tam o' Shanter* (*see* page 140). Captain Francis Grose, an antiquarian and an artist, was in Scotland to collect material for a book of drawings, *Antiquities of Scotland*, which he published in 1789-91. He met Burns at Robert Riddel's house, Friars Carse, and the two got on famously. Grose was a fat and jolly man with a fund of good stories, whose company Burns relished. At Burns' suggestion, Grose was to include in his book a drawing of the ruined Alloway Kirk where Burns' father was buried, and the poet agreed to write an accompanying poem based on a local 'witch story': the result was *Tam o' Shanter*.

Burns outlined the story on which his poem is based in a letter to Captain Grose: 'On a market day in the town of Ayr, a farmer from Carrick, and consequently whose way lay by the very gate of Alloway kirk-yard, in order to cross the river Don at the old bridge, which is about two or three hundred yards farther on than the said gate, had been detained by his business till by the time he reached Alloway, it was the wizard hour, between night and morning.

'Though he was terrified with a blaze streaming from the kirk, yet as it is a well known fact, that to turn back on these occasions is running by far the greatest risk of mis-chief, he prudently advanced on his road. When he reached the gate of the kirk-yard, he was surprised and en-tertained, through the ribs and arches of an old gothic window which still faces the highway, to see a dance of witches merrily footing it around their old sooty black-guard master, who was keeping them all alive with the power of his bagpipe. The farmer stopping his horse to observe them a little, could plainly descry the faces of many old women of his acquaintance and neighbourhood. How the gentleman was dressed, tradition does not say; but the ladies were all in their smocks; and one of them hap-pening unluckily to have a smock which was considerably too short to answer all the purpose of that piece of dress, our farmer was so tickled that he involuntarily burst out, with a loud laugh. 'Weel luppen, Maggy wi' the short sark!' and recollecting himself, instantly spurred his horse to the top of his speed.

'I need not mention the universally known fact that no diabolical power can pursue you beyond the middle of a running stream. Lucky it was for the poor farmer that the river Doon was so near, for notwithstanding the speed of his horse, which was a good one, against he reached the middle of the arch of the bridge, and consequently the middle of the stream, the pursuing, vengeful hags were so close at his heels, that one of them actually sprung to seize him: but it was too late; nothing was on her side of the stream but the horse's tail, which immediately gave way to her infernal grip, as if blasted by a stroke of lightning; but the farmer was beyond her reach.'

Most critics agree that *Tam o' Shanter* is Burns' finest work. It contains all the best natural qualities of his verse. The poet himself held this opinion. According to his wife, Burns wrote the poem in a single day after a walk along the banks of the Nith. There may have been an element of truth in this as Burns had long been in the habit of composing in his head while walking, riding or labouring in the fields. But Burns was aware of the real work which went into fine writing., and this was shown when he commented, 'all my poetry is the effect of easy composition, but of laborious correction.' And again, 'Though the rough material of fine writing is undoubtedly the gift of genius, the workmanship is as certainly the united effort of labour, attention and pains.' In a letter to Mrs Dunlop dated April 1791, Burns described *Tam o' Shanter* half-jokingly as his 'standard performance in the poetical line', and as showing 'a force of genius and a finishing polish that I despair of

ever excelling'. The poem was first published in two Edinburgh periodicals in March 1791. It came out in Grose's
Antiquities of Scotland a month later.

Burns now had many friends of his own choosing in and
around Dumfries, particularly among the townsfolk. He
also continued to be treated like a celebrity and entertained
in the homes of the gentry, although here he was never really accepted as an equal. Class barriers were maintained,
and Burns, although he enjoyed flattery and attention as
well as any man, always felt himself to be on show. This
irritated him and sometimes led him into acts of indiscre-
tion which over the years have been recorded and commented upon at the expense of the more solid virtues of his
life among his true friends and family and at work.

His early biographers suggested that he behaved badly
and began flirting with other women in Dumfries but this
is almost certainly untrue. There are no suggestions that he
was unhappy with Jean; he was a caring and affectionate
father and he worked hard. As an exciseman he won promotion, and, apart from minor upsets, pleased his employers. It is true that his sympathies with revolutionary causes
accounted for some embarrassment and an official investigation into his political position. The trouble was that
Burns was incapable of hiding his real emotions.

One of his firmest friends from Dumfries days, John
Syme, recollected how Burns' face showed his every emo-
tion: 'The poet's expression varied perpetually, according
to the idea that predominated in his mind: and it was beautiful to mark how well the play of his lips indicated the sen-

timent he was about to utter. His eyes and lips, the first remarkable for fire, and the second for flexibility, formed at all times an index to his mind.' That Burns was an open and generous man cannot be denied. On countless occasions he is seen helping out relatives and friends with advice, with support and with money. Such generosity and steadfastness were not always returned to him in his hours of need.

In May 1793, Burns and Jean moved to a larger self-contained house in Mill Vennel, Dumfries, and were able to enjoy a more comfortable existence in a home big enough to accommodate their growing family. Earlier that year, on 18 February, Creech had published a new edition of Burns' poems in Edinburgh which included *Tam o' Shanter*. The fourth volume of Johnson's *Scots Musical Museum* had been published the year before, and soon afterwards Burns received a letter from George Thomson, who held a junior clerical post in Edinburgh, inviting him to collaborate in a new collection of Scottish songs.

It was an invitation Burns could not resist, and for the rest of his life he devoted his spare time to providing Thomson with over a hundred songs. He didn't claim any payment for his work and was very much offended when, after publication of the first part of *Select Scottish Airs* in June 1793, Thomson sent him five pounds. (It was a measure of how desperate things were to become for Burns that, a few days before his death, he pleaded with Thomson to send another five pounds to help him out.) One of the songs in Thomson's collection was 'Scots, Wha Hae' (*see*

page 160), which has become one of Scotland's two national songs—the other, 'Auld Lang Syne' (*see* page 201),
was published after Burns' death in the fifth volume of
Johnson's *Musical Museum*.

In one of his letters to Thomson, Burns sets out his
method of writing songs: 'Until I am complete master of a
tune in my own singing (such as it is) I can never compose
for it. My way is this. I consider the poetic Sentiment correspondent to my idea of the musical expression; then I
choose my theme; begin one Stanza; when that is composed, which is generally the most difficult part of the
business, I walk out, sit down now and then, look out for
objects in Nature round me that are in unison or harmony
with the cogitations of my fancy and workings of my
bosom, humming every now and then the air with the
verses I have framed. . . .'

Burns' health worsened but he remained active in pur-
suit of his excise duties. The war with France had cut down
his income because of lost perquisites from import duties,
and he was constantly worried about money matters and
falling behind with his rent. He was tempted to abandon
the excise service altogether and accept an offer from the
London *Morning Chronicle*, made in May 1794, to become
an occasional correspondent at a salary of five guineas a
week. He did not, principally because the newspaper job
meant he would have to live in London and he was always
suspicious of earning a living by writing.

A woman called Maria Riddel was important to Burns
during his final years. Her friendship brought him intellec-

tual stimulus as well as romance. Burns wrote to Maria Riddel in spring 1795 saying that he was 'so ill as to be scarce able to hold this miserable pen to this miserable paper'. In September, his daughter Elizabeth died after a long illness and the heartbroken Burns could not even attend her funeral because of the demands of his excise duties. He suffered a severe attack of what he called rheumatic fever, and his friend and doctor, James Maxwell, recommended that he should take a break away from his work and go to the coast to take some gentle exercise and sea bathing. That the doctor's advice propelled Burns to his grave seems undeniable.

At the little hamlet of Brow on the Solway coast near Dumfries, Burns dutifully waded out each day over the sands into the cold sea, water up to his armpits. The 'cure' did nothing to help his condition. As he wrote in a letter to George Thomson soon after he arrived at Brow, ' . . . my health being so precarious, nay dangerously situated, that as a last effort I am here at sea-bathing quarters. Besides my inveterate rheumatism, my appetite is quite gone, and I am so emaciated as to be scarce able to support myself on my own legs . . . .'

Maria Riddel happened to be staying near Brow when Burns was there, and she invited him to dinner. 'I was struck,' she writes, 'with his appearance on entering the room. The stamp of death was impressed on his features. He seemed already touching the brink of eternity. His first salutation was "Well, Madam, have you any commands for the other world?" '

'Well, Madam, have you any commands for the other world?'

His final letter, written after his return to Dumfries, was to his father-in-law: 'Do for Heaven's sake, send Mrs Armour here immediately. My wife is hourly expecting to be put to bed. Good God! What a situation for her to be in, poor girl, without a friend! I returned from sea-bathing quarters today, and my medical friends would almost persuade me I am better; but I think and feel that my strength is so gone that the disorder will prove fatal to me.'

At five o'clock on the morning of Thursday 21 July 1796, Burns died, just at the time when he might have expected promotion to be an Excise Collector and, as he put it, 'a life of literary leisure with a decent competence'. He was thirty-seven years of age. Burns was given a military-style funeral by his friends, the Dumfries Volunteers firing three volleys over his grave. Meanwhile, Jean was giving birth to her ninth child whom she had christened Maxwell in honour of the doctor who had sent poor Burns to plunge himself into the sea water at Brow. On 25 July, Burns was buried in St Michael's Churchyard, Dumfries.

Land of Burns

MANY of the places where Robert Burns lived and worked may be visited. A number of sites have been acquired by the National Trust for Scotland, and others have been preserved and enhanced by the local authority in cooperation with the Scottish Tourist Board. Anyone wishing to know more of Burns and the Land o' Burns should visit or write to the Scottish Tourist Board in Edinburgh. The Board publishes a number of attractive pamphlets on Burns and is responsible for developing The Burns Heritage Trail, a tour of the places linked with Scotland's greatest poet: some of these are listed here.

Alloway The cottage where Robert Burns was born still stands and can be visited. Joined to the house is a museum with a major collection of relics. Alloway Kirk, where Tam o' Shanter saw the witches dance, is about half a mile from the cottage and was already a ruin in Burns' day. William Burnes, the poet's father, is buried here. Nearby is the Land o' Burns Centre developed by the local authority and the Scottish Tourist Board. Its displays and audiovisual shows bring to life the works and times of Burns. The Auld Brig o' Doon, which crosses the river, is believed to be 700 years old. It is the bridge over which Tam made his escape from the witches. Alongside is the Burns Monument, completed in 1823, which contains more relics of the poet.

Ayr Burns' statue stands outside the railway station, and nearby, in the High Street, is the Tam o' Shanter Inn (now a museum) which is the starting point for Tam's ride. The Auld Brig mentioned in the poem *The Brigs of Ayr* (not included in this selection) is still in use for pedestrians. The house in Sandgate where young Robert was tutored for three weeks by John Murdoch is commemorated by a tablet. Burns was baptised at the Auld Kirk in Ayr.

Brow The little hamlet on the Solway Coast which in Burns' time had an unfounded reputation as a spa. Shortly before he died, Burns was sent here by his doctor and friend, James Maxwell, in the hope that sea-bathing might be beneficial to his health.

Dumfries The ancient Bridge House and the Burgh Museum have relics of the poet. Burns' first Dumfries home in the Wee Vennel (now Bank Street) is not open to the public. His second and larger home in Mill Vennel (now Burns Street) is a leading Burns Museum. His wife, Jean Armour, lived here until her death in 1834. Burns was buried in St Michael's Churchyard. On 19 September 1815, his remains were transferred to a vault under a mausoleum erected to his memory. The churchyard holds numerous graves of Burns' friends. In a narrow passage leading off the High Street is the Globe Inn, described by Burns as his 'fa-

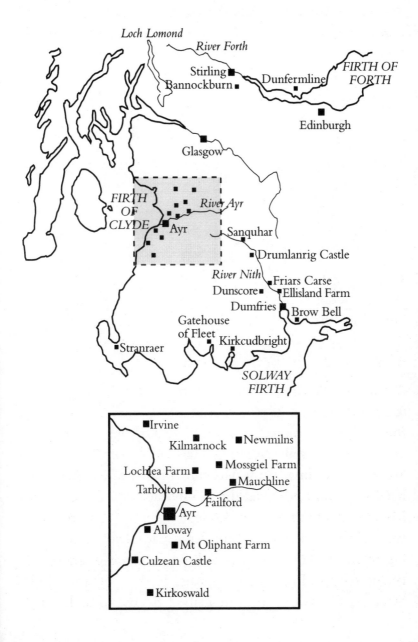

vourite howff'. The relics include his chair and an in-scribed window pane. The Theatre Royal, visited frequently by Burns, has been reconstructed.

Burns' second and larger home at Dumfries in Mill Vennel

Eglinton Woods Off the main road between Irvine and Kilwinning, are Eglinton Castle, Park and Woods (which cover 50 acres), owned and maintained by the local authority. There is a small statue of Burns in the park, supposedly marking the spot where Richard Brown urged Burns to send his verses to a magazine for publication.

Ellisland Farm This hundred-acre farm to which Burns moved in June 1788 is on the west bank of the Nith about six miles north of Dumfries on the A76. Ellisland was farmed until 1921, when it was bought by a former president of the Edinburgh Burns Club and given to the nation.

It is preserved as a working farm and the restored granary includes an exhibition that gives a vivid image of Burns' life as a farmer and shows how he tried to introduce new farming methods.

Failford Due south of Lochlea on the A758 is a memorial to Burns' 'Highland Mary' (Mary Campbell of Auchnamore). It is in the centre of the village at the conjectured spot over the Fail Water where Burns and Mary parted for the last time with an exchange of vows.

Gatehouse of Fleet In the Murray Arms Hotel a room may be seen where Burns probably wrote 'Scots, Wha Hae'.

Irvine Here Robert and Gilbert Burns went in 1781 to learn flax dressing. They lodged in a house in Glasgow Vennel, now marked by a plaque. The Irvine Burns Club, founded 2 June 1826, is one of the oldest in the world and has a very interesting museum. Two of its founder members were personal friends of Burns: Dr John MacKenzie and David Sillar. The club rooms are situated in a house called Wellwood in Eglinton Street and are open to the public.

Kilmarnock Here the first Kilmarnock edition of Burns' poems was published by John Wilson; the site of his premises is marked by a plaque. Dean Castle, formerly the home of Burns' friend, the Earl of Glencairn, now has an attractive garden and a notable collection of musical instruments. In Kay Park, the Burns Monument is a red sandstone temple surmounted by a tower which contains a good museum of Burnsiana.

Kirkcudbright In the Selkirk Arms Inn it is believed Burns wrote the Selkirk Grace, still sometimes used:

> Some ha'e meat and canna eat,
> And some wad eat that want it,
> But we ha'e meat and we can eat
> Sae let the Lord be Thankit.

Kirkoswald Souter Johnnie's House, built in 1785, is a National Trust for Scotland property. It is a museum with furniture of Burns' day and the implements of a village cobbler. In the garden are four amusing life-size figures of Tam o' Shanter, Souter Johnnie, the innkeeper and his wife. They were made in 1802 by James Thom, a self-taught sculptor from Tarbolton.

Largs An unusual monument to the bard is the Burns Garden at Douglas Park which has been laid out in an attempt to retell the story of the life and works of the great Scottish poet. One part of the garden relates the tale of Tam o' Shanter and there are replicas of famous Alloway landmarks.

Lochlea Farm This farm was the home of the Burns family from 1777 until 1784 and it lies about a mile north of the B744, halfway between Tarbolton and Mauchline. The present buildings are not the ones lived in by Burns.

Mauchline A major centre of Burns interest. Burns is said to have met Jean Armour on the green by Mauchline Burn. Burns House, a museum in Castle Street, is where he took a room for Jean in 1788 and where the couple lived for a few months before the move to Ellisland. Burns and Jean were married in Gavin Hamilton's house which adjoins the fifteenth-century tower of Mauchline Castle. Auld Nanse Tinnock's Tavern (now no longer an inn) is opposite. Mauchline Churchyard (the present church was built in 1829) contains the graves of four of Burns' children and some of his friends, including Gavin Hamilton and Willie Fisher (Holy Willie). Opposite the church is Poosie Nansie's Tavern, an ale shop and lodging house in Burns' time. You can still have a drink there. The revels witnessed by Burns resulted in the poem *The Jolly Beggars*. On the outskirts of the town, at the junction of the A76 and the B744 stands the National Burns Memorial Tower in which there is a small museum.

Poosie Nansie's Tavern in Mauchline

Mossgiel Farm The farm rented by the Burns brothers in 1783. At the Burns National Memorial, fork left on to the Tarbolton road and the farm, which has since been rebuilt, is on the right.

Mount Oliphant William Burnes moved here with his family in 1766. The farm, which is still worked today but with a neighbouring farm, stands on high ground one and a half miles southeast of Alloway. It commands magnificent views of Arran and the Ayrshire coast.

Tarbolton Here is the seventeenth-century house, now owned by the National Trust for Scotland, where Burns attended dancing classes in 1779, founded with his friends The Bachelors' Club in 1780 and was installed as a mason in 1781. Willie's Mill (Tarbolton Mill) is just outside Tarbolton on the road to Lochlea. In Burns' day it was the home of his close friend William Muir. When Jean Armour was thrown out of her home because of her association with Burns she found shelter with Muir. It was also the setting for Burns' satirical poem 'Death and Doctor Hornbrook' (not included in this selection).

Poems and Songs

THE TWA DOGS

*The Twa Dogs is a poem with social comment. It is a conversa-
tion between a rich dog called Caesar, and a poor dog called
Luath, with the unexpected twist that Caesar makes the case for
the poor, while Luath is more willing to accept his circumstances.
Luath was the name of a dog of Burns' who was killed in a fight
the night before his father's death; Burns said that he would im-
mortalise him. Caesar is an imaginary creation.*

A TALE

'Twas in that place o' Scotland's isle
That bears the name o' auld King Coil,
Upon a bonie day in June,
When wearing through the afternoon,
Twa dogs, that were na thrang at hame,
Forgathered ance upon a time.
    The first I'll name, they ca'd him Caesar,
Was keepit for 'his Honor's' pleasure:
His hair, his size, his mouth, his lugs,
Show'd he was nane o' Scotland's dogs;
But whalpit some place far abroad,
Whare sailors gang to fish for cod.
    His locked, letter'd, braw brass collar
Show'd him the gentleman an' scholar;
But though he was o' high degree,
The fient a pride, nae pride had he;

But wad hae spent an hour caressin',
Ev'n wi' a tinkler-gipsy's messin;
At kirk or market, mill or smiddie,
Nae tawted tyke, though e'er sae duddie,
But he wad stand, as glad to see him,
An' stroan'd on stanes an' hillocks wi' him.
   The tither was a ploughman's collie—
A rhyming, ranting, raving billie,
Wha for his friend an' comrade had him,
And in his freaks had Luath ca'd him,
After some dog in Highland sang,
Was made lang syne—Lord knows how lang.
   He was a gash an' faithfu' tyke,
As ever lap a sheugh or dyke.
His honest, sonsie, baws'nt face
Ay gat him friends in ilka place;
His breast was white, his tousie back
Weel clad wi' coat o' glossy black;
His gawsie tail, wi' upward curl,
Hung owre his hurdies wi' a swirl.
   Nae doubt but they were fain o' ither,
And unco pack an' thick thegither;
Wi' social nose whyles snuff'd an' snowkit;
Whyles mice an' moudieworts they howkit;
Whyles scour'd awa' in lang excursion,
An' worry'd ither in diversion;
Till tir'd at last wi' monie a farce,
They sat them down upon their arse,
An' there began a lang digression
About the 'lords o' the creation'.

Caesar

I've aften wonder'd, honest Luath,
What sort o' life poor dogs like you have;
An' when the gentry's life I saw,
What way poor bodies liv'd ava.

Our laird gets in his racked rents,
His coals, his kain, an' a' his stents:
He rises when he likes himsel;
His flunkies answer at the bell;
He ca's his coach; he ca's his horse;
He draws a bonie silken purse,
As lang's my tail, whare, through the steeks,
The yellow letter'd Geordie keeks.

Frae morn to e'en it's nought but toiling,
At baking, roasting, frying, boiling;

An' though the gentry first are stechin,
Yet ev'n the ha' folk fill their pechan
Wi' sauce, ragouts, an sic like trashtrie,
That's little short o' downright wastrie:
Our whipper-in, wee, blastit wonner,
Poor, worthless elf, it eats a dinner,
Better than onie tenant-man
His Honor has in a' the lan';
An' what poor cot-folk pit their painch in,
I own it's past my comprehension.

LUATH

Trowth, Caesar, whyles they're fash't eneugh:
A cotter howkin in a sheugh,
Wi' dirty stanes biggin a dyke,
Baring a quarry, an' sic like;
Himsel, a wife, he thus sustains,
A smytrie o' wee duddie weans,
An' nought but his han' darg to keep
Them right an' tight in thack an' rape.

An' when they meet wi' sair disasters,
Like loss o' health or want o' masters,
Ye maist wad think, a wee touch langer,
An' they maun starve o' cauld and hunger:
But how it comes, I never kend yet,
They're maistly wonderfu' contented;
An' buirdly chiels, an' clever hizzies,
Are bred in sic a way as this is.

CAESAR

But then to see how ye're negleckit,

How huff'd an' cuff'd an' disrespeckit!
Lord man, our gentry care as little
For delvers, ditchers, an' sic cattle;
They gang as saucy by poor folk,
As I wad by a stinking brock.

I've notic'd, on our laird's court-day,
(An' monie a time my heart's been wae),
Poor tenant bodies, scant o' cash,
How they maun thole a factor's snash:
He'll stamp an threaten, curse an' swear
He'll apprehend them, poind their gear;
While they maun staun', wi' aspect humble,
An' hear it a', an' fear an' tremble!

I see how folk live that hae riches;
But surely poor-folk maun be wretches!

LUATH

They're nae sae wretched's ane wad think:
Though constantly on poortith's brink,
They're sae accustom'd wi' the sight,
The view o't gies them little fright.

Then chance an' fortune are sae guided,
They're ay in less or mair provided;
An' though fatigu'd wi' close employment,
A blink o' rest's a sweet enjoyment.

The dearest comfort o' their lives,
Their grushie weans an' faithfu' wives;
The prattling things are just their pride,
That sweeten a' their fire-side.

An' whyles twalpennie worth o'nappy

Can mak the bodies unco happy:
They lay aside their private cares,
To mind the Kirk and State affairs;
They'll talk o' patronage an' priests,
Wi' kindling fury i' their breasts,
Or tell what new taxation's comin,
An' ferlie at the folk in Lon'on.

As bleak-fac'd Hallowmass returns,
They get the jovial, ranting kirns,
When rural life, of ev'ry station,
Unite in common recreation;
Love blinks, Wit slaps, an' social Mirth
Forgets there's Care upo' the earth.

That merry day the year begins,
They bar the door on frosty win's;
The nappy reeks wi' mantling ream,
An' sheds a heart-inspiring steam;
The luntin pipe, an' sneeshin mill,
Are handed round wi' right guid will;
The cantie auld folks crackin crouse,
The young anes ranting through the house—
My heart has been sae fain to see them,
That I for joy hae barkit wi' them.

Still it's owre true that ye hae said
Sic game is now owre aften play'd;
There's monie a creditable stock
O' decent, honest, fawsont folk,
Are riven out baith root an' branch,
Some rascal's pridefu' greed to quench,
Wha thinks to knit himsel the faster

In favor wi' some gentle master,
Wha, aiblins thrang a parliamentin',
For Britain's guid his saul indentin'—

CAESAR

Haith, lad, ye little ken about it:
For Britain's guid! guid faith! I doubt it.
Say rather, gaun as Premiers lead him:
An' saying aye or no's they bid him:
At operas an' plays parading,
Mortgaging, gambling, masquerading:
Or maybe, in a frolic daft,
To Hague or Calais taks a waft,
To mak a tour an' tak a whirl,
To learn *bon ton*, an' see the worl'.
There, at Vienna or Versailles,
He rives his father's auld entails;
Or by Madrid he taks the rout,
To thrum guitars an' fecht wi' nowt;
Or down Italian vista startles,
Whore-hunting amang groves o' myrtles
Then bowses drumlie German-water,
To mak himself look fair an' fatter,
An' purge the bitter ga's an' cankers
O' curst Venetian bores an' chancres.
For Britain's guid! for her destruction!
Wi' dissipation, feud an' faction.

LUATH

Hech man! dear sirs! is that the gate
They waste sae monie a braw estate!

Are we sae foughten an' harass'd
For gear to gang that gate at last?
   O would they stay aback frae courts,
An' please themsels wi' countra sports,
It wad for ev'ry ane be better,
The laird, the tenant, an' the cotter!
For thae frank, rantin, ramblin billies,
Fient haet o' them's ill-hearted fellows:
Except for breakin o' their timmer,
Or speakin lightly o' their limmer,
Or shootin of a hare or moor-cock,
The ne'er-a-bit they're ill to poor folk.
   But will ye tell me, master Caesar:
Sure great folk's life's a life o' pleasure?
Nae cauld nor hunger e'er can steer them,
The vera thought o't need na fear them.

CAESAR

   Lord, man, were ye but whyles whare I am,
The gentles, ye wad ne'er envy 'em!
   It's true, they need na starve or sweat,
Through winter's cauld, or simmer's heat;
They've nae sair wark to craze their banes,
An' fill auld-age wi' grips an' granes:
But human bodies are sic fools,
For a' their colleges an' schools,
That when nae real ills perplex them,
They mak enow themsels to vex them;
An' ay the less they hae to sturt them,
In like proportion, less will hurt them.

A countra fellow at the pleugh,
His acre's till'd, he's right eneugh;
A countra girl at her wheel,
Her dizzen's done, she's unco weel;
But gentlemen, an' ladies warst,
Wi' ev'n-down want o' wark are curst:
They loiter, lounging, lank an' lazy;
Though deil-haet ails them, yet uneasy;
Their days insipid, dull an' tasteless;
Their nights unquiet, lang an' restless.

An' ev'n their sports, their balls an' races,
Their gallowping through public places,
There's sic parade, sic pomp an' art,
The joy can scarcely reach the heart.

The men cast out in party-matches,
Then sowther a' in deep debauches;
Ae night they're mad wi' drink an' whoring,
Niest day their life is past enduring.

The ladies arm-in-arm in clusters,
As great an' gracious a' as sisters;
But hear their absent thought o' ither,
They're a' run deils an' jads thegither.
Whyles, owre the wee bit cup an' platie,
They sip the scandal-potion pretty;
Or lee-lang nights, wi' crabbit leuks
Pore owre the devil's pictur'd beuks;
Stake on a chance a farmer's stackyard,
An' cheat like onie unhang'd blackguard.

There's some exceptions, man an' woman;
But this is Gentry's life in common.

By this, the sun was out o' sight,
An' darker gloamin brought the night;
The bum-clock humm'd wi' lazy drone;
The kye stood rowtin' i' the loan;
When up they gat, an' shook their lugs,
Rejoic'd they were na men, but dogs;
An' each took aff his several way,
Resolv'd to meet some ither day.

THE JOLLY BEGGARS

LOVE AND LIBERTY – A CANTATA

The Jolly Beggars, *a poem made up of a collection of songs, was inspired by a visit the poet made to Poosie Nansie's Tavern in Mauchline, where a group of beggars were enjoying themselves one night, full of drink and song. Each song is sung by a different character in the tavern—notice how the construction of the verses of each song varies. There are several references in the soldier's song that may not be familiar to modern readers: 'the heights of Abram' refers to the battlefield near Quebec where General Wolfe defeated the French in 1759 but was killed; 'Moro' refers to the capture of Havana, the capital of Cuba, by the British in 1762 (Moro was the castle at the city's entrance); 'Curtis' is Admiral Roger Curtis who took part in the lifting of the seige of Gibraltar by the Spanish and French forces in 1782; 'Elliot' is General George Elliot who defended Gibraltar. 'Kilbaigie' in the tinker's song (which begins 'My bonnie lass, I work in brass') refers to a type of whisky distilled at the Kilbaigie distillery, that was popular in Poosie Nansie's Tavern.*

RECITATIVO

When lyart leaves bestrow the yird,
Or, wavering like the bauckie-bird,
    Bedim cauld Boreas' blast;
When hailstanes drive wi' bitter skyte,
And infant frosts begin to bite,
    In hoary cranreuch drest;

Ae night at e'en a merry core
O' randie, gangrel bodies
   In Poosie-Nansie's held the splore,
   To drink their orra duddies:
     Wi' quaffing and laughing
      They ranted an' they sang,
     Wi' jumping an' thumping
      The vera girdle rang.

First, niest the fire, in auld red rags
Ane sat, weel brac'd wi' mealy bags
   And knapsack a' in order;
His doxy lay within his arm;
Wi' usquebae an' blankets warm,
   She blinket on her sodger.
An' ay he gies the tozie drab
   The tither skelpin kiss,
While she held up her greedy gab
   Just like an aumous dish:
     Ilk smack still did crack still
      Like onie cadger's whup;
     Then, staggering an' swaggering,
      He roar'd this ditty up:—

SONG

TUNE: *Soldier's Joy*

I am a son of Mars, who have been in many wars,
   And show my cuts and scars wherever I come:
This here was for a wench, and that other in a
   trench,

When welcoming the French at the sound of
the drum.

My prenticeship I past, where my leader breath'd
his last,
When the bloody die was cast on the heights
of Abram;
I served out my trade when the gallant game
was play'd,
And the Moro low was laid at the sound of
the drum.

I lastly was with Curtis among the floating batt'ries,
And there I left for witness an arm and a limb;
Yet let my country need me, with Eliott to lead me
I'd clatter on my trumps at the sound of the
drum.

And now, though I must beg with a wooden arm
and leg,
And many a tatter'd rag hanging over my bum,
I'm as happy with my wallet, my bottle, and my
callet
As when I us'd in scarlet to follow a drum.

What though with hoary locks I must stand the winter
shocks,
Beneath the woods and rocks oftentimes for a
home?
When the tother bag I sell, and the tother
bottle tell,
I could meet a troop of Hell at the sound of a
drum.

RECITATIVO

He ended; and the kebars sheuk
        Aboon the chorus roar;
While frighted rattons backward leuk,
        An' seek the benmost bore:
A fairy fiddler frae the neuk,
        He skirl'd out *Encore!*
But up arose the martial chuck,
        An' laid the loud uproar:—

SONG

TUNE: *Sodger Laddie*

I once was a maid, though I cannot tell when,
        And still my delight is in proper young men.
Some one of a troop of dragoons was my daddie:
        No wonder I'm fond of a sodger laddie!

The first of my loves was a swaggering blade:
        To rattle the thundering drum was his trade;
His leg was so tight, and his cheek was so ruddy,
        Transported I was with my sodger laddie.

But the godly old chaplain left him in the lurch;
        The sword I forsook for the sake of the church;
He ventured the soul, and I risket the body:
        'Twas then I prov'd false to my sodger laddie.

Full soon I grew sick of my sanctified sot;
        The regiment at large for a husband I got;
From the gilded spontoon to the fife I was ready
        I asked no more but a sodger laddie.

But the Peace it reduc'd me to beg in despair,

Till I met my old boy in a Cunningham Fair;
His rags regimental they flutter'd so gaudy:
　　My heart it rejoic'd at a sodger laddie.

And now I have liv'd—I know not how long!
　　But still I can join in a cup and a song;
And whilst with both hands I can hold the glass steady,
　　Here's to thee, my hero, my sodger laddie!

RECITATIVO

Poor Merry-Andrew in the neuk,
　　Sat guzzling wi' a tinkler-hizzie;
They mind't na wha the chorus teuk,
　　Between themselves they were sae busy.
At length, wi' drink an' courting dizzy,
　　He stoiter'd up an' made a face;
Then turn'd, an' laid a smack on Grizzie,
　　Syne tun'd his pipes wi' grave grimace:—

SONG

TUNE: *Auld Sir Symon*

Sir Wisdom's a fool when he's fou;
　　Sir Knave is a fool in a session:
He's there but a prentice I trow,
　　But I am a fool by profession.

My grannie she bought me a beuk,
　　An' I held awa to the school:
I fear I my talent misteuk,
　　But what will ye hae of a fool?

For drink I wad venture my neck;

A hizzie's the half of my craft:
But what could ye other expect
 Of ane that's avowedly daft?

I ance was tyed up like a stirk,
 For civilly swearing and quaffing;
I ance was abus'd i' the kirk
 For towsing a lass i' my daffin.

Poor Andrew that tumbles for sport
 Let naebody name wi' a jeer:
There's even, I'm tauld, i' the Court
 A tumbler ca'd the Premier.

Observ'd ye yon reverend lad
 Mak faces to tickle the mob?
He rails at our mountebank squad—
 It's ravalship just i' the job!

And now my conclusion I'll tell,
 For faith! I'm confoundedly dry:
The chiel that's a fool for himsel,
 Guid Lord! he's far dafter than I.

RECITATIVO

Then niest outspak a raucle carlin,
Wha kent fu' weel to cleek the sterlin',
For monie a pursie she had hooked,
An' had in monie a well been douked.
Her love had been a Highland laddie,
But weary fa' the waefu' woodie!
Wi' sighs an' sobs she thus began
To wail her braw John Highlandman:—

SONG

TUNE: *O, An Ye Were Dead, Guidman*

A Highland lad my love was born,
The lalland laws he held in scorn,
But he still was faithfu' to his clan,
My gallant, braw John Highlandman.

Chorus

Sing hey my braw John Highlandman!
Sing ho my braw John Highlandman!
There's not a lad in a' the lan'
Was match for my John Highlandman!

With his philibeg, an' tartan plaid,
An' guid claymore down by his side,
The ladies' hearts he did trepan,
My gallant, braw John Highlandman.

We ranged a' from Tweed to Spey,
An' liv'd like lords an' ladies gay,
For a lalland face he feared none,
My gallant, braw John Highlandman.

They banish'd him beyond the sea,
But ere the bud was on the tree,
Adown my cheeks the pearls ran,
Embracing my John Highlandman.

But Och! they catch'd him at the last,
And bound him in a dungeon fast.

My curse upon them every one—
They've hang'd my braw John
    Highlandman!

And now a widow I must mourn
The pleasures that will ne'er return;
No comfort but a hearty can
When I think on John Highlandman.

Chorus

Sing hey my braw John Highlandman!
Sing ho my braw John Highlandman!
There's not a lad in a' the lan'
Was match for my John Highlandman!

RECITATIVO

A pigmy scraper on a fiddle,
Wha us'd to trystes an' fairs to driddle,
Her strappin limb an' gawsie middle
        (He reach'd nae higher)
Had hol'd his heartie like a riddle,
        An' blawn't on fire.

Wi' hand on hainch and upward e'e,
He croon'd his gamut, one, two, three,
Then in an *arioso* key
        The wee Apollo
Set off wi' *allegretto* glee
        His *giga* solo:—

SONG

TUNE: *Whistle Owre the Lave O't*

Let me ryke up to dight that tear;
　　An' go wi' me an' be my dear,
An' then your every care an' fear
　　May whistle owre the lave o't.

Chorus

I am a fiddler to my trade,
An' a' the tunes that e'er I play'd,
The sweetest still to wife or maid
　　Was Whistle Owre the Lave O't.

At kirns an' weddins we'se be there,
An' O, sae nicely 's we will fare!
We'll bowse about till Daddie Care
　　Sing *Whistle Owre the Lave O't.*

Sae merrily the banes we'll pyke,
An' sun oursels about the dyke;
An' at our leisure, when ye like,
　　We'll—whistle owre the lave o't!

But bless me wi' your heav'n o' charms,
An' while I kittle hair on thairms,
Hunger, cauld, an' a' sic harms
　　May whistle owre the lave o't.

Chorus

I am a fiddler to my trade,
An' a' the tunes that e'er I play'd
The sweetest still to wife or maid
　　Was Whistle Owre the Lave O't.

RECITATIVO

Her charms had struck a sturdy caird
    As weel as poor gut-scraper;
He taks the fiddler by the beard,
    An' draws a roosty rapier;
He swoor by a' was swearing worth
    To speet him like a pliver,
Unless he would from that time forth
    Relinquish her for ever.

Wi' ghastly e'e poor Tweedle-Dee
    Upon his hunkers bended,
An' pray'd for grace wi' ruefu' face,
    An' sae the quarrel ended.
But though his little heart did grieve
    When round the tinkler prest her,
He feign'd to snirtle in his sleeve
    When thus the caird address'd her:—

SONG

TUNE: *Clout the Cauldron*

My bonie lass, I work in brass,
    A tinkler is my station;
I've travell'd round all Christian ground
    In this my occupation;
I've taen the gold, an' been enrolled
    In many a noble squadron;
But vain they search'd when off I march'd
    To go an' clout the cauldron.

Despise that shrimp, that wither'd imp,

With a' his noise an' cap'rin,
An' take a share wi' those that bear
    The budget and the apron!
And by that stowp, my faith an' houpe!
    And by that dear Kilbaigie!
If e'er ye want, or meet wi' scant,
    May I ne'er weet my craigie!

RECITATIVO

The caird prevail'd: th' unblushing fair
    In his embraces sunk,
Partly wi' love o'ercome sae sair,
    An' partly she was drunk.
Sir Violino, with an air
    That show'd a man o' spunk,
Wish'd unison between the pair,
    An' made the bottle clunk
        To their health that night.

But hurchin Cupid shot a shaft,
    That play'd a dame a shavie:
The fiddler rak'd her fore and aft
    Behint the chicken cavie;
Her lord, a wight of Homer's craft
    Though limpin' wi' the spavie,
He hirpl'd up, an lap like daft,
    An' shor'd them 'Dainty Davie'
        O' boot that night.

He was a care-defying blade
    As ever Bacchus listed!

Though Fortune sair upon him laid,
   His heart, she ever miss'd it.
He had no wish but—to be glad,
   Nor want but—when he thristed,
He hated nought but—to be sad;
   An' thus the Muse suggested
         His sang that night:—

SONG

TUNE: *For A' That, An' A' That'*

I am a Bard, of no regard
   Wi' gentle folks an' a' that,
But Homer-like the glowrin byke,
   Frae town to town I draw that.

Chorus

For a' that, an' a' that,
   An' twice as muckle's a' that,
I've lost but ane, I've twa behin',
   I've wife eneugh for a' that.

I never drank the Muses' stank,
   Castalia's burn, an' a' that;
But there is streams, an' richly reams—
   My Helicon I ca' that.

Great love I bear to a' the fair,
   Their humble slave an' a' that;
But lordly will, I hold it still
   A mortal sin to thraw that.

In raptures sweet this hour we meet
    Wi' mutual love an' a' that;
But for how lang the flie may stang,
    Let inclination law that!

Their tricks an' craft hae put me daft,
    They've taen me in, an' a' that;
But clear your decks, an' here's the Sex!
    I like the jads for a' that.

Chorus

For a' that, an' a' that
    An' twice as muckle's a' that,
My dearest bluid, to do them guid,
    They're welcome till't for a' that!

RECITATIVO

So sung the Bard, and Nansie's wa's
Shook with a thunder of applause,
    Re-echo'd from each mouth!
They toom'd their pocks, they pawn'd their duds,
They scarcely left to coor their fuds,
    To quench their lowin drouth.
Then owre again the jovial thrang
    The Poet did request
To lowse his pack, an' wale a sang,
A ballad o' the best:
    He rising, rejoicing
        Between his twa Deborahs,
    Looks round him, an' found them
        Impatient for the chorus:—

SONG

TUNE: *Jolly Mortals, Fill Your Glasses*

See the smoking bowl before us!
  Mark our jovial, ragged ring!
Round and round take up the chorus,
  And in raptures let us sing:

Chorus

A fig for those by law protected!
  Liberty's a glorious feast,
Courts for cowards were erected,
  Churches built to please the priest!

What is title, what is treasure,
  What is reputation's care?
If we lead a life of pleasure,
  'Tis no matter how or where!

With the ready trick and fable
  Round we wander all the day;
And at night in barn or stable
  Hug our doxies on the hay.

Does the train-attended carriage
  Through the country lighter rove?
Does the sober bed of marriage
  Witness brighter scenes of love?

Life is all a variorum,
  We regard not how it goes;
Let them prate about decorum,
  Who have character to lose.

Here's to budgets, bags and wallets!
   Here's to all the wandering train!
Here's our ragged brats and callets!
   One and all, cry out, Amen!

Chorus

A fig for those by law protected!
   Liberty's a glorious feast,
Courts for cowards were erected,
   Churches built to please the priest!

SCOTCH DRINK

This poem is a eulogy (a verse in praise of something or someone) to whisky—Burns instils it with magical properties. In the nineteenth verse, 'Forbes' of Culloden had been allowed to distil whisky free of duty (tax) at his barony of Ferintosh. This privilege was abolished in 1785.

> *Gie him strong drink until he wink,*
> *That's sinking in despair;*
> *An' liquor guid to fire his bluid,*
> *That's prest wi' grief an' care:*
> *There let him bowse, and deep carouse,*
> *Wi' bumpers flowing o'er,*
> *Till he forgets his loves or debts,*
> *An' minds his griefs no more.*
>
> SOLOMON'S PROVERBS, 31: 6, 7.

Let other poets raise a frácas
'Bout vines, an' wines, an' drucken Bacchus,
An' crabbit names an' stories wrack us,
                    An' grate our lug:
I sing the juice Scotch bear can mak us,
                    In glass or jug.

O thou, my Muse! guid auld Scotch drink!
Whether through wimplin worms thou jink,
Or, richly brown, ream owre the brink,
                    In glorious faem,
Inspire me, till I lisp an' wink,
                    To sing thy name!

Let husky wheat the haughs adorn,
An' aits set up their awnie horn,
An' pease an' beans, at e'en or morn,
    Perfume the plain:
Leeze me on thee, John Barleycorn,
     Thou king o' grain!

On thee aft Scotland chows her cood,
In souple scones, the wale o' food!
Or tumbling in the boiling flood
    Wi' kail an' beef;
But when thou pours thy strong heart's blood,
     There thou shines chief.

Food fills the wame, an' keeps us leevin';
Though life's a gift no worth receivin,
When heavy-dragg'd wi' pine an' grievin;
    But oil'd by thee,
The wheels o' life gae down-hill, scrievin,
     Wi' rattlin glee.

Thou clears the head o' doited Lear,
Thou cheers the heart o' drooping Care;
Thou strings the nerves o' Labour sair,
    At's weary toil;
Thou ev'n brightens dark Despair
    Wi' gloomy smile.

Aft, clad in massy siller weed,
Wi' gentles thou erects thy head;
Yet, humbly kind in time o' need,
    The poor man's wine:

His wee drap parritch, or his bread,
                    Thou kitchens fine.

Thou art the life o' public haunts:
But thee, what were our fairs and rants?
Ev'n godly meeting o' the saunts,
                    By thee inspir'd,
When, gaping, they besiege the tents,
                    Are doubly fir'd.

That merry night we get the corn in,
O sweetly, then, thou reams the horn in!
Or reekin on a New-Year mornin
                    In cog or bicker,
An' just a wee drap spiritual burn in,
                    An' gusty sucker!

When Vulcan gies his bellows breath,
An' ploughmen gather wi' their graith,
O rare! to see thee fizz an' freath
                    I' th' lugget caup!
Then Burnewin comes on like death
                    At ev'ry chaup.

Nae mercy, then, for airn or steel:
The brawnie, bainie, ploughman chiel,
Brings hard owrehip, wi' strudy wheel,
                    The strong forehammer,
Till block an' studdie ring an' reel,
                    Wi' dinsome clamour.

When skirlin weanies see the light,
Thou maks the gossips clatter bright,
How fumbling cuifs their dearies slight;

Wae worth the name!
Nae howdie gets a social night,
          Or plack frae them.

When neebors anger at a plea,
An' just as wud as wud can be,
How easy can the barley-brie
          Cement the quarrel!
It's ay the cheapest lawyer's fee,
          To taste the barrel.

Alake! that e'er my Muse has reason,
To wyte her countrymen wi' treason!
But monie daily weet their weason
          Wi' liquors nice,
An' hardly, in a winter season,
          E'er spier her price.

Wae worth that brandy, burnin trash!
Fell source o' monie a pain an' brash!
Twins monie a poor, doylt, drucken hash,
          O' half his days;
An' sends, beside, auld Scotland's cash
          To her warst faes.

Ye Scots, wha wish auld Scotland well!
Ye chief, to you my tale I tell,
Poor, plackless devils like mysel!
          It sets you ill,
Wi' bitter, dearthfu' wines to mell,
          Or foreign gill.

May gravels round his blather wrench,
An' gouts torment him, inch by inch,

Wha twists his gruntle wi' a glunch
        O' sour disdain,
Out owre a glass o' whisky–punch
        Wi' honest men!

O Whisky! soul o' plays an' pranks!
Accept a Bardie's gratefu' thanks!
When wanting thee, what tuneless cranks
        Are my poor verses!
Thou comes—they rattle i' their ranks
        At ithers' arses!

Thee, Ferintosh! O sadly lost!
Scotland lament frae coast to coast!
Now colic grips, an' barkin hoast
        May kill us a';
For loyal Forbés chartered boast
        Is taen awa!

Thae curst horse-leeches o' th' Excise,
Wha mak the whisky stells their prize!
Haud up thy han', Deil! ance, twice, thrice!
        There, seize the blinkers!
An' bake them up in brunstane pies
        For poor damn'd drinkers.

Fortune! if thou'll but gie me still
Hale breeks, a scone, an' whisky gill,
An' rowth o' rhyme to rave at will,
        Tak a' the rest,
An' deal't about as thy blind skill
        Directs thee best.

The Author's Earnest Cry and Prayer

Addressed to the 'chosen five and forty' Scottish representatives in the 'Muckle House' (the House of Commons), the poem mentions the politicians of the day by name. The poet eloquently and humorously attacks excise duty on whisky, Scotland's 'aqua vitae', water of life. This poem was written before the Scotch Distilleries Act of 1786 which abolished tax on drink and put a tax on stills.

TO THE SCOTCH REPRESENTATIVES
IN THE HOUSE OF COMMONS

Dearest of distillation! last and best—
How art thou lost!—

PARODY ON MILTON

Ye Irish lords, ye knights an' squires,
Wha represent our brughs an' shires,
An' doucely manage our affairs
   In Parliament,
To you a simple Bardie's prayers
   Are humbly sent.

Alas! my roupet Muse is haerse!
Your Honors' hearts wi' grief 'twad pierce,
To see her sittin on her arse
   Low i' the dust,
And scriechin out prosaic verse,
   An' like to brust!

Tell them wha hae the chief direction,
Scotland an' me's in great affliction,
E'er sin' they laid that curst restriction
            On aqua-vitae;
An' rouse them up to strong conviction,
            An' move their pity.

Stand forth, an' tell yon Premier youth
The honest, open, naked truth:
Tell him o' mine an' Scotland's drouth,
            His servants humble:
The muckle deevil blaw you south,
            If ye dissemble!

Does onie great man glunch an' gloom?
Speak out, an' never fash your thumb!
Let posts an' pensions sink or soom
            Wi' them wha grant 'em:
If honestly they canna come,
            Far better want 'em.

In gath'rin votes you were na slack;
Now stand as tightly by your tack:
Ne'er claw your lug, an' fidge your back,
            An' hum an haw;
But raise your arm, an' tell your crack
            Before them a'.

Paint Scotland greetin owre her thrissle;
Her mutchkin stowp as toom's a whissle;
An' damn'd excisemen in a bustle,
            Seizin a stell,

Triumphant, crushin't like a mussel,
              Or lampit shell!

Then, on the tither hand, present her—
A blackguard smuggler right behint her,
An' cheek-for-chow, a chuffie vintner
              Colleaguing join,
Pickin her pouch as bare as winter
              Of a' kind coin.

Is there, that bears the name o' Scot,
But feels his heart's bluid rising hot,
To see his poor auld mither's pot
              Thus dung in staves,
An' plunder'd o' her hindmost groat,
              By gallows knaves?

Alas! I'm but a nameless wight,
Trode i' the mire out o' sight!
But could I like Montgomeries fight,
              Or gab like Boswell,
There's some sark-necks I wad draw tight,
              An' tie some hose well.

God bless your Honors! can ye see't,
The kind, auld, cantie carlin greet,
An' no get warmly to your feet,
              An' gar them hear it,
An' tell them wi' a patriot-heat,
              Ye winna bear it?

Some o' you nicely ken the laws,
To round the period an' pause,

An' with rhetoric clause on clause
              To mak harangues:
Then echo through Saint Stephen's wa's
              Auld Scotland's wrangs.

Dempster, a true blue Scot I'se warran;
Thee, aith-detesting, chaste Kilkerran;
An' that glib-gabbet Highland baron,
              The Laird o' Graham;
An' ane, a chap that's damn'd auldfarran,
              Dundas his name:

Erskine, a spunkie Norland billie;
True Campbells, Frederick and Ilay;
An' Livistone, the bauld Sir Willie;
              An' monie ithers,
Whom auld Demosthenes or Tully
              Might own for brithers.

Thee sodger Hugh, my watchman stented,
If Bardies e'er are represented;
I ken if that your sword were wanted,
              Ye'd lend your hand;
But when there's ought to say anent it,
              Ye're at a stand.

Arouse, my boys! exert your mettle,
To get auld Scotland back her kettle;
Or faith! I'll wad my new pleugh-pettle,
              Ye'll see't or lang,
She'll teach you, wi' a reekin whittle,
              Anither sang.

This while she's been in crankous mood,
Her lost Militia fir'd her bluid;
(Deil na they never mair do guid,
                              Play'd her that pliskie!)
An' now she's like to rin red-wud
                              About her whisky.

An' Lord! if ance they pit her till't
Her tartan petticoat she'll kilt,
An' durk an' pistol at her belt,
                              She'll tak the streets,
An' rin her whittle to the hilt,
                              I' the first she meets!

For God-sake, sirs! then speak her fair,
An' straik her cannie wi' the hair,
An' to the Muckle House repair,
                              Wi' instant speed,
An' strive, wi' a' your wit an' lear,
                              To get remead.

Yon ill-tongue'd tinkler, Charlie Fox,
May taunt you wi' his jeers an' mocks;
But gie him't het, my hearty cocks!
                              E'en cowe the cadie!
An' send him to his dicing box
                              An' sportin lady.

Tell you guid bluid of auld Boconnock's,
I'll be his debt twa mashlum bonnocks,
An' drink his health in auld Nanse Tinnock's
                              Nine times a-week.

If he some scheme, like tea an' winnocks,
                    Wad kindly seek.

Could he some commutation broach,
I'll pledge my aith in guid braid Scotch,
He needna fear their foul reproach
                    Nor erudition,
Yon mixtie-maxtie, queer hotch-potch,
                    The Coalition.

Auld Scotland has a raucle tongue;
She's just a devil wi' a rung;
An' if she promise auld or young
                    To tak their part,
Though by the neck she should be strung,
                    She'll no desert.

And now, ye chosen Five-and-Forty,
May still your mither's heart support ye;
Then, though a minister grow dorty,
                    An' kick your place,
Ye'll snap your fingers, poor an' hearty,
                    Before his face.

God bless your Honors, a' your days,
Wi' sowps o' kail and brats o' claes,
In spite o' a' the thievish kaes,
                    That haunt, St Jamie's!
Your humble Bardie sings an' prays,
                    While Rab his name is.

POSTSCRIPT

Let half-starv'd slaves in warmer skies
See future wines, rich-clust'ring, rise;
Their lot auld Scotland ne'er envies,
    But, blythe and frisky,
She eyes her freeborn, martial boys
    Tak aff their whisky.

What though their Phœbus kinder warms,
While fragrance blooms and Beauty charms,
When wretches range, in famish'd swarms,
    The scented groves;
Or, hounded forth, dishonor arms
    In hungry droves!

Their gun's a burden on their shouther;
They downa bide the stink o' powther;
Their bauldest thought's a hank'ring swither
    To stan' or rin,
Till skelpt—a shot—they're aff, a' throw'ther,
    To save their skin.

But bring a Scotsman frae his hill,
Clap in his cheek a Highland gill,
Say, such is royal George's will,
    An' there's the foe!
He has nae thought but how to kill
    Twa at a blow.

Nae cauld, faint-hearted doubtings tease him;
Death comes, wi' fearless eye he sees him;

Wi' bluidy han' a welcome gies him;
    An' when he fa's,
His latest draught o' breathin lea'es him
    In faint huzzas.

Sages their solemn een may steek
An' raise a philosophic reek,
An' physically causes seek
    In clime an' season;
But tell me whisky's name in Greek:
    I'll tell the reason.

Scotland, my auld, respected mither!
Though whiles ye moistify your leather,
Till whare ye sit on craps o' heather
    Ye tine your dam,
Freedom and whisky gang thegither,
    Tak aff your dram!

To a Mouse

ON TURNING HER UP IN HER NEST
WITH THE PLOUGH, NOVEMBER 1785

To a Mouse *was probably composed as Burns worked at the
plough (it is said that he did much of his composition this way)
and is inspired by a real incident. The poet's mood expresses his
doubts about the future and regrets about the past. It may in some
way have been influenced by the death of his ten-year-old brother
John the month before, and the death of his father the previous
year.*

Wee, sleekit, cowrin, tim'rous beastie,
O' what a panic's in thy breastie!
Thou need na start awa sae hasty
   Wi' bickering brattle!
I wad be laith to rin an' chase thee,
   Wi' murd'ring pattle!

I'm truly sorry man's dominion
Has broken Nature's social union,
An' justifies that ill opinion
   Which makes thee startle
At me, thy poor, earth-born companion
   An' fellow mortal!

I doubt na, whyles, but thou may thieve;
What then? poor beastie, thou maun live!
A daimen icker in a thrave
   'S a sma' request;
I'll get a blessin wi' the lave,
   An' never miss't!

Thy wee-bit housie, too, in ruin!
Its silly wa's the win's are strewin!
An' naething, now, to big a new ane,
O' foggage green!
An' bleak December's win's ensuin,
Baith snell an' keen!

Thou saw the fields laid bare an' waste,
An' weary winter comin fast,
An' cozie here, beneath the blast,
Thou thought to dwell,
Till crash! the cruel coulter past
Out through thy cell.

That wee bit heap o' leaves an' stibble,
Has cost thee monie a weary nibble!

Now thou's turned out, for a' thy trouble,
                But house or hald,
To thole the winter's sleety dribble,
                An' cranreuch cauld!

But Mousie, thou art no thy lane,
In proving foresight may be vain:
The best-laid schemes o'mice an' men
                Gang aft agley,
An' lea'e us nought but grief an' pain,
                For promis'd joy!

Still thou art blest, compared wi' me!
The present only toucheth thee:
But och! I backward cast my e'e,
                On prospects drear!
An' forward, though I canna see,
                I guess an' fear!

THE DEATH AND DYING WORDS OF POOR MAILIE

THE AUTHOR'S ONLY PET YOWE:
AN UNCO MOURNFU' TALE

This and the following poem are mock elegies (mournful poems dedicated to the dead) written in 1783, inspired by a real incident. Burns had bought a ewe and two lambs from a neighbour and the ewe was tied up in a field at their farm in Lochlea. The sheep got tangled up and fell into a ditch. Robert is said to have composed the sheep's dying words as he returned from working with the plough in the evening.

As Mailie, an' her lambs thegither
Were ae day nibblin on the tether,
Upon her cloot she coost a hitch,
An' owre she warsl'd in the ditch:
There, groanin, dying, she did lie,
When Hughoc he cam doytin by.

   Wi' glowrin een, an' lifted han's
Poor Hughoc like a statue stan's;
He saw her days were near-hand ended,
But, wae's my heart! he could na mend it!
He gapèd wide, but naething spak.
At length poor Mailie silence brak:—

   'O thou, whase lamentable face
Appears to mourn my woefu' case!

My dying words attentive hear,
An' bear them to my master dear.

'Tell him, if e'er again he keep
As muckle gear as buy a sheep—
O, bid him never tie them mair,
Wi' wicked strings o' hemp or hair!
But ca' them out to park or hill,
An' let them wander at their will:
So may his flock increase, an' grow
To scores o' lambs, an' packs o' woo'!

'Tell him, he was a master kin',
An' ay was guid to me an' mine;
An' now my dying charge I gie him,
My helpless lambs, I trust them wi' him.

'O, bid him save their harmless lives,
Frae dogs, an' tods, an' butchers' knives!
But gie them guid cow-milk their fill,
Till they be fit to fend themsel;
An' tent them duly, e'en an' morn,
Wi' teats o' hay an' ripps o' corn.

'An' may they never learn the gaets,
Of ither vile, wanrestfu' pets—
To slink through slaps, an' reave an' steal,
At stacks o' pease, or stocks o' kail!
So may they, like their great forbears,
For monie a year come through the shears:
So wives will gie them bits o' bread,
An' bairns greet for them when they're dead.

'My poor toop-lamb, my son an' heir,
O, bid him breed him up wi' care!
An' if he live to be a beast,
To pit some havins in his breast!
An' warn him—what I winna name—
To stay content wi' yowes at hame;
An' no to rin an' wear his cloots,
Like other menseless, graceless brutes.

'An' neist, my yowie, silly thing;
Gude keep thee frae a tether string!
O, may thou ne'er forgather up,
Wi' onie blastit, moorland toop;
But ay keep mind to moop an' mell,
Wi' sheep o' credit like thysel!

'And now, my bairns, wi' my last breath,
I lea'e my blessin wi' you baith:
An' when you think upo' your mither,
Mind to be kind to ane anither.

'Now, honest Hughoc, dinna fail,
To tell my master a' my tale;
An' bid him burn this cursed tether,
An' for thy pains thou'se get my blether.'
This said, poor Mailie turn'd her head,
An' clos'd her een amang the dead!

Poor Mailie's Elegy

Lament in rhyme, lament in prose,
Wi' saut tears tricklin down your nose;
Our Bardie's fate is at a close,
      Past a' remead!
The last, sad cape-stane of his woes;
      Poor Mailie's dead!

It's no the loss of warl's gear,
That could sae bitter draw the tear,
Or mak our Bardie, dowie, wear
      The mourning weed:
He's lost a friend an' neebor dear
      In Mailie dead.

Through a' the toun she trotted by him;
A lang half-mile she could descry him;
Wi' kindly bleat, when she did spy him,
      She ran wi' speed:
A friend mair faithfu' ne'er cam nigh him,
      Than Mailie dead.

I wat she was a sheep o' sense,
An' could behave hersel wi' mense:
I'll say't, she never brak a frence,
      Through thievish greed.
Our Bardie, lanely, keeps the spence
      Sin' Mailie's dead.

Or, if he wanders up the howe,
Her livin image in her yowe
Comes bleatin till him, owre the knowe,
    For bits o' bread;
An' down the briny pearls rowe
    For Mailie dead.

She was nae get o' moorlan tips,
Wi' tawted ket, an' hairy hips;
For her forbears were brought in ships,
    Frae 'yont the Tweed:
An bonier fleesh ne'er cross'd the clips
    Than Mailie's dead.

Wae worth the man wha first did shape
That vile, wanchancie thing—a rape!
It maks guid fellows girn an' gape,
    Wi' chokin dread;
An' Robin's bonnet wave wi' crape
    For Mailie dead.

O a' ye bards on bonie Doon!
An' wha an Ayr your chanters tune!
Come, join the melancholious croon
    O' Robins's reed!
His heart will never get aboon!
    His Mailie's dead!

To a Mountain Daisy

ON TURNING ONE DOWN WITH THE PLOUGH
IN APRIL 1786

*The poet regrets having had to kill a flower in the field that he is
ploughing. He recognises its beauty and the struggle it has had to
survive, and compares this to the human condition: that we will all
one day meet a similar fate and perhaps just as unfairly.*

Wee, modest, crimson-tipped flow'r,
Thou's met me in an evil hour;
For I maun crush amang the stoure
    Thy slender stem:
To spare thee now is past my pow'r,
    Thou bonie gem.

Alas! it's no thy neebor sweet,
The bonie lark, companion meet,
Bending thee 'mang the dewy weet,
    Wi' spreckl'd breast!
When upward-springing, blythe, to greet
    The purpling east.

Cauld blew the bitter-biting north
Upon thy early, humble birth;
Yet cheerfully thou glinted forth
    Amid the storm,
Scarce rear'd above the parent-earth
    Thy tender form

The flaunting flow'rs our gardens yield,
High shelt'ring woods and wa's maun shield;
But thou, beneath the random bield
    O' clod or stane,
Adorns the histie stibble-field,
      Unseen, alane.

There, in thy scanty mantle clad,
Thy snawie bosom sun-ward spread,
Thou lifts thy unassuming head
    In humble guise;
But now the share uptears thy bed,
      And low thou lies!

Such is the fate of artless maid,
Sweet flow'ret of the rural shade!
By love's simplicity betray'd,
    And guileless trust;
Till she, like thee, all soil'd, is laid
      Low i' the dust.

Such is the fate of simple Bard,
On Life's rough ocean luckless starr'd!
Unskilful he to note the card
    Of prudent lore,
Till billows range, and gales blow hard,
      And whelm him o'er.

Such fate to suffering Worth is giv'n,
Who long with wants and woes has striv'n,
By human pride or cunning driv'n
    To mis'ry's brink;

Till, wrench'd or ev'ry stay but Heav'n,
  He, ruin'd, sink!

Ev'n thou who mourn'st the Daisy's fate,
That fate is thine—no distant date;
Stern Ruin's plough-share drives elate,
  Full on thy bloom,
Till crush'd beneath the furrow's weight
  Shall be thy doom!

THE VISION

The poet comments that if he had not spent his youth writing poetry he might have been rich. He is visited by his muse (his inspiration to write), who in this instance takes a physical form and has the name of Coila. She brings him a poetic vision of Scotland and chastises him for wishing he had not taken up poetry.

The poem mentions several eminent Scots and events of Scottish history. 'His Country's Saviour', mentioned in the the eighteenth verse, refers to William Wallace; 'Richardton' is Adam Wallace of Richardton, William's kinsman; 'Sark' refers to the victory on the banks of the Sark in 1448 where Wallace, laird of Craigie, fought valiantly and was fatally injured; 'Brydone's brave ward' in verse twenty-two refers to an explorer called Colonel Fullarton who had accompanied Patrick Brydone, a once celebrated traveller, on an expedition; 'Dempster', mentioned in the twenty-ninth verse, is Dempster of Dunnichen, a parliamentary patriot who is also mentioned in the Author's Earnest Cry and Prayer *(see page 97).*

DUAN FIRST

The sun had clos'd the winter day,
The curlers quat their roaring play,
And hunger'd maukin taen her way,
   To kail-yards green,
While faithless snaws ilk step betray
    Whare she has been.

The thresher's weary flingin-tree,
The lee-lang day had tired me;

And when the day had clos'd his e'e,
                    Far i' the west,
Ben i' the spence, right pensivelie,
                    I gaed to rest.

There, lanely by the ingle-cheek,
I sat and ey'd the spewing reek,
That fill'd, wi hoast-provoking smeek,
                    The auld clay biggin;
An' heard the restless rattons squeak
                    About the riggin.

All in this mottie, misty clime,
I backward mus'd on wasted time:
How I had spent my youthfu' prime,
                    An' done naething,
But stringing blethers up in rhyme,
                    For fools to sing.

Had I to guid advice but harkit,
I might, by this, hae led a market,
Or strutted in a bank and clarkit
                    My cash-account:
While here, half-mad, half-fed, half-sarkit,
                    Is a' th' amount.

I started, mutt'ring 'Blockhead! coof!'
An' heav'd on high my waukit loof,
To swear by a' yon starry roof,
                    Or some rash aith,
That I henceforth would be rhyme-proof
                    Till my last breath—

When click! the string the snick did draw;
And jee! the door gaed to the wa';
And by my ingle-lowe I saw,
                         Now bleezin bright,
A tight, outlandish hizzie, braw,
                         Come full in sight.

Ye need na doubt, I held my whisht;
The infant aith, half-form'd, was crusht;
I glowr'd as eerie's I'd been dusht,
                         In some wild glen;
When sweet, like modest Worth, she blusht,
                         And stepped ben.

Green, slender, leaf-clad holly-boughs
Were twisted, gracefu', round her brows;
I took her for some Scottish Muse,
                         By that same token;
And come to stop those reckless vows,
                         Would soon been broken.

A 'hair-brain'd, sentimental trace'
Was strongly marked in her face;
A widly-witty, rustic grace
                         Shone full upon her;
Her eye, ev'n turn'd on empty space,
                         Beam'd keen with honor.

Down flow'd her robe, a tartan sheen,
Till half a leg was scrimply seen;
And such a leg! my bonie Jean
                         Could only peer it;

Sae straught, saw taper, tight an' clean
                    Nane else came near it.

Her mantle large, of greenish hue,
My gazing wonder chiefly drew;
Deep lights and shades, bold–mingling, threw
                    A lustre grand;
And seem'd, to my astonish'd view,
                    A well-known land.

Here, rivers in the sea were lost;
There, mountains to the skies were toss't;
Here, tumbling billows mark'd the coast
                    With surging foam;
There, distant shone Art's lofty boast,
                    The lordly dome.

Here, Doon pour'd down his far-fetch'd
    floods;
There, well-fed Irwine stately thuds:
Auld hermit Ayr staw through his woods,
                    On to the shore;
And many a lesser torrent scuds
                    With seeming roar.

Low, in a sandy valley spread
An ancient borough rear'd her head;
Still, as in Scottish story read,
                    She boasts a race
To ev'ry nobler virtue bred,
                    And polish'd grace.

By stately tow'r, or palace fair,
Or ruins pendent in the air,
Bold stems of heroes, here and there,
                    I could discern;
Some seem'd to muse, some seem'd to dare
                    With feature stern.

My heart did glowing transport feel,
To see a race heroic wheel,
And brandish round the deep-dyed steel
                    In sturdy blows;
While, back-recoiling, seem'd to reel
                    Their suthron foes.

His Country's Saviour, mark him well!
Bold Richardton's heroic swell;
The chief, on Sark who glorious fell
                    In high command;
And he whom ruthless fates expel
                    His native land.

There, where a sceptr'd Pictish shade
Stalk'd round his ashes lowly laid,
I mark'd a martial race, pourtray'd
                    In colours strong:
Bold, soldier-featur'd, undismay'd,
                    They strode along.

Through many a wild, romantic grove,
Near many a hermit-fancied cove
(Fit haunts for friendship or for love
                    In Musing mood),

An aged Judge, I saw him rove,
                    Dispensing good.

With deep-struck, reverential awe,
The learned Sire and Son I saw;
To Nature's God, and Nature's law,
                    They gave their lore;
This, all its source and end to draw,
                    That, to adore.

Brydon's brave ward I well could spy,
Beneath old Scotia's smiling eye;
Who call'd on Fame, low standing by,
                    To hand him on,
Where many a patriot-name on high,
                    And hero shone.

DUAN SECOND

With musing-deep, astonish'd stare,
I view'd the heavenly-seeming Fair;
A whisp'ring throb did witness bear
                    Of kindred sweet,
When with an elder sister's air
                    She did me greet.

'All hail! my own inspired Bard!
In me thy native Muse regard!
Nor longer mourn thy fate is hard
                    Thus poorly low!
I come to give thee such reward,
                    As we bestow.

'Know, the great Genius of this land
Has many a light aerial band,
Who, all beneath his high command,
                    Harmoniously,
As arts or arms they understand,
                    Their labours ply.

'They Scotia's race among them share:
Some fire the soldier on to dare;
Some rouse the patriot up to bare
                    Corruption's heart;
Some teach the bard—a darling care—
                    The tuneful art.

''Mong swelling floods of reeking gore,
They, ardent, kindling spirits pour;
Or, 'mid the venal senate's roar,
                    They, sightless, stand,
To mend the honest patriot-lore,
                    And grace the hand.

'And when the bard, or hoary sage,
Charm or instruct the future age,
They bind the wild poetic rage
                    In energy;
Or point the inconclusive page
                    Full on the eye.

'Hence, Fullarton, the brave and young;
Hence, Dempster's zeal-inspired tongue;
Hence, sweet, harmonious Beattie sung
                    His *Minstrel* lays,

Or tore, with noble ardour stung,
                    The sceptic's bays.

'To lower orders are assign'd
The humbler ranks of human-kind,
The rustic bard, the laboring hind,
                    The artisan;
All chuse, as various they're inclin'd,
                    The various man.

'When yellow waves the heavy grain,
The threat'ning storm some strongly rein,
Some teach to meliorate the plain,
                    With tillage-skill;
And some instruct the shepherd-train,
                    Blythe o'er the hill.

'Some hint the lover's harmless wile;
Some grace the maiden's artless smile;
Some soothe the laborer's weavy toil
                    For humble gains,
And make his cottage-scenes beguile
                    His cares and pains.

'Some, bounded to a district-space,
Explore at large man's infant race,
To mark the embryotic trace
                    Of rustic bard;
And careful note each opening grace,
                    A guide and guard.

'Of these am I—Coila my name:
And this district as mine I claim,

Where once the Campbells, chiefs of fame,
                    Held ruling pow'r:
I mark'd thy embryo-tuneful flame,
                    Thy natal hour.

'With future hope I oft would gaze,
Fond, on thy little early ways:
Thy rudely caroll'd, chiming phrase,
                    In uncouth rhymes;
Fir'd at the simple, artless lays
                    Of other times.

'I saw thee seek the sounding shore,
Delighted with the dashing roar;
Or when the North his fleecy store
                    Drove through the sky,
I saw grim Nature's visage hoar
                    Struck thy young eye.

'Or when the deep green-mantled earth
Warm cherish'd ev'ry flow'ret's birth,
And joy and music pouring forth
                    In ev'ry grove;
I saw thee eye the gen'ral mirth
                    With boundless love.

'When ripen'd fields and azure skies
Call'd forth the reaper's rustling noise,
I saw thee leave their ev'ning joys,
                    And lonely stalk,
To vent thy bosom's swelling rise,
                    In pensive walk.

'When youthful Love, warm-blushing, strong,
Keen-shivering, shot thy nerves along,
Those accents grateful to thy tongue,
              Th' adored *Name,*
I taught thee how to pour in song
              To soothe thy flame.

'I saw thy pulse's maddening play,
Wild send thee Pleasure's devious way,
Misled by Fancy's meteor-ray,
              By passion driven;
But yet the light that led astray
              Was light from Heaven.

'I taught thy manners-painting strains
The loves, the ways of simple swains,
Till now, o;er all my wide domains
              Thy fame extends;
And some, the pride of Coila's plains,
              Become thy friends.

'Thou canst not learn, nor can I show,
To paint with Thomson's landscape glow;
Or wake the bosom-melting throe
              With Shenstone's art;
Or pour, with Gray, the moving flow
              Warm on the heart.

'Yet, all beneath th' unrivall'd rose,
The lowly daisy sweetly blows;
Though large the forest's monarch throws
              His army-shade,

Yet green the juicy hawthorn grows
    Adown the glade.

'Then never murmur nor repine;
Strive in thy humble sphere to shine;
And trust me, not Potosi's mine,
    Nor king's regard,
Can give a biss o'ermatching thine,
    A rustic Bard.

'To give my counsels all in one:
Thy tuneful flame still careful fan;
Preserve the dignity of Man,
    With soul erect;
And trust the Universal Plan
    Will all protect.

'An wear thou *this*'—she solemn said,
And bound the holly round my head:
The polish'd leaves and berries red
    Did rustling play;
And, like a passing thought, she fled
    In light away.

The Cotter's Saturday Night

The Cotter's Saturday Night *is an idealistic depiction of a night in the household of a farmer and his family. The cotter himself is inspired by the poet's own father, William Burnes. The R. Aitken in the inscription was a fellow writer and a great friend of Burns'.*

INSCRIBED TO R AITKEN, ESQ.

> *Let not Ambition mock their useful toil,*
> *Their homely joys, and destiny obscure;*
> *Nor Grandeur hear, with a disdainful smile,*
> *The short and simple annals of the poor.*
>
> GRAY

My lov'd, my honor'd, much respected friend!
  No mercenary bard his homage pays;
With honest pride, I scorn each selfish end,
  My dearest meed, a friend's esteem and praise:
  To you I sing, in simple Scottish lays,
The lowly train in life's sequester'd scene;
  The native feelings strong, the guileless ways;
What Aiken in a cottage would have been;
Ah! though his worth unknown, far happier there
    I ween!

November chill blaws loud wi' angry sugh;
  The short'ning winter-day is near a close;
The miry beasts retreating frae the pleugh;
  The black'ning trains o' craws to their repose:
  The toil-worn Cotter frae his labor goes—

This night his weekly moil is at an end,
    Collects his spades, his mattocks, and his hoes,
Hoping the morn in ease and rest to spend,
And weary, o'er the moor, his course does hameward
        bend.

At length his lonely cot appears in view,
    Beneath the shelter of an aged tree;
Th' expectant wee-things, toddlin, stacher through
    To meet their dad, wi' flichterin' noise and glee.
    His wee bit ingle, blinkin bonilie,
His clean hearth-stane, his thrifty wifie's smile,
    The lisping infant, prattling on his knee,
Does a' his weary carking cares beguile,
And makes him quite forget his labor and his toil.

Belyve, the elder bairns come drappin in,
    At service out, amang the farmers roun';
Some ca' the pleugh, some herd, some tentie rin
    A cannie errand to a neibor town:
    Their eldest hope, their Jenny, woman grown,
In youthfu' bloom, love sparkling in her e'e,
    Comes hame; perhaps, to shew a braw new gown,
Or deposite her sair-won penny-fee,
To help her parents dear, if they in hardship be.

With joy unfeign'd, brothers and sisters meet,
    And each for other's weelfare kindly spiers:
The social hours, swift-wing'd, unnotic'd fleet;
    Each tells the uncos that he sees or hears.
    The parents partial eye their hopeful years;
Anticipation forward points the view;

The mother, wi' her needle and her sheers,
Gars auld claes look amaist as weel's the new;
The father mixes a' wi' admonition due.

Their master's and their mistress's command
    The younkers a' are warned to obey;
And mind their labors wi' an eydent hand,
    And ne'er, though out o' sight, to jauk or play:
    'And O! be sure to fear the Lord alway,
And mind your duty, duly, morn and night;
    Lest in temptation's path ye gang astray,
Implore His counsel and assisting might:
They never sought in vain that sought the Lord aright.'

But hark! a rap comes gently to the door;
    Jenny, wha kens the meaning o' the same,
Tells how a neebor lad came o'er the moor,
    To do some errands, and convey her hame.
    The wily mother sees the conscious flame
Sparkle in Jenny's e'e, and flush her cheek;
    With heart-struck anxious care, enquires his name,
While Jenny hafflins is afraid to speak;
Weel-pleas'd the mother hears, it's nae wild,
        worthless rake.

With kindly welcome, Jenny brings him ben;
    A strappin' youth, he takes the mother's eye;
Blythe Jenny sees the visit's no ill ta'en;
    The father cracks of horses, pleughs, and kye.
    The youngster's artless heart o'erflows wi' joy,
But blate and laithfu', scarce can weel behave;
    The mother, wi' a woman's wiles, can spy

What makes the youth sae bashfu' and sae grave;
Weel-pleas'd to think her bairn's respected like the lave.

O happy love! where love like this is found:
    O heart-felt raptures! bliss beyond compare!
I've paced much this weary, mortal round,
    And sage experience bids me this declare:—
    'If Heaven a draught of heavenly pleasure spare,
One cordial in this melancholy vale,
    'Tis when a youthful, loving, modest pair,
In other's arms, breathe out the tender tale

Beneath the milk-white thorn that scents the ev'ning
    gale.'

Is there, in human form, that bears a heart,
    A wretch! a villain! lost to love and truth!
That can, with studied, sly, ensnaring art,
    Betray sweet Jenny's unsuspecting youth?
      Curse on his perjur'd arts! dissembling, smooth!
Are honor, virtue, conscience, all exil'd?
    Is there no pity, no relenting ruth,
Points to the parents fondling o'er their child?
Then paints the ruin'd maid, and their distraction wild?

But now the supper crowns their simple board,
    The halesome parritch, chief o' Scotia's food;
The soupe their only hawkie does afford,
    That, 'yont the hallan snugly chows her cood;
      The dame brings forth, in complimental mood,
To grace the lad, her weel-hain'd kebbuck, fell;
    And aft he's prest, and aft he ca's it guid;
The frugal wifie, garrulous, will tell,
How 'twas a towmond auld, sin' lint was i' the bell.

The cheerfu' supper done, wi' serious face,
    They, round the ingle, form a circle wide;
The sire turns o'er, wi' patriarchal grace,
    The big ha'-Bible, ance his father's pride.
      His bonnet rev'rently is laid aside,
His lyart haffets wearing thin and bare;
    Those strains that once did sweet in Zion glide,
He wales a portion with judicious care,
And 'Let us worship God!' he says, with solemn air.

They chant their artless notes in simple guise,
    They tune their hearts, by far the noblest aim;
Perhaps *Dundee's* wild-warbling measures rise,
    Or plaintive *Martyrs*, worthy of the name;
    Or noble *Elgin* beets the heaven-ward flame,
The sweetest far of Scotia's holy lays:
    Compar'd with these, Italian trills are tame;
The tickl'd ears no heart-felt raptures raise;
Nae unison hae they, with our Creator's praise.

The priest-like father reads the sacred page,
    How Abram was the friend of God on high;
Or, Moses bade eternal warfare wage
    With Amalek's ungracious progeny;
    Or, how the royal Bard did groaning lie
Beneath the stroke of Heaven's avenging ire;
    Or Job's pathetic plaint, and wailing cry;
Or rapt Isaiah's wild, seraphic fire;
Or other holy seers that tune the sacred lyre.

Perhaps the Christian volume is the theme:
    How guiltless blood for guilty man was shed;
How He, who bore in Heaven the second name,
    Had not on earth whereon to lay His head;
    How His first followers and servants sped;
The precepts sage they wrote to many a land:
    How he, who lone in Patmos banished,
Saw in the sun a mighty angel stand,
And heard great Bab'lon's doom pronounc'd by
        Heaven's command.

Then kneeling down to Heaven's Eternal King,

The saint, the father, and the husband prays:
Hope 'springs exulting on triumphant wing.'
    That thus they all shall meet in future days,
    There, ever bask in uncreated rays,
No more to sigh or shed the bitter tear,
    Together hymning their Creator's praise,
In such society, yet still more dear;
While circling Time moves round in an eternal sphere.

Compar'd with this, how poor Religion's pride,
    In all the pomp of method, and of art;
When men display to congregations wide
    Devotion's ev'ry grace, except the heart!
    The Power, incens'd, the pageant will desert,
The pompous strain, the sacerdotal stole:
    But haply, in some cottage far apart,
May hear, well-pleas'd, the language of the soul,
And in His Book of Life the inmates poor enroll.

Then homeward all take off their sev'ral way;
    The youngling cottagers retire to rest:
The parent-pair their secret homage pay,
    And proffer up to Heaven the warm request,
    That He who stills the raven's clam'rous nest,
And decks the lily fair in flow'ry pride,
    Would, in the way His wisdom sees the best,
For them and for their little ones provide;
But, chiefly, in their hearts with Grace Divine preside.

From scenes like these, old Scotia's grandeur springs
    That makes her lov'd at home, rever'd abroad:
Princes and lords are but the breath of kings,

'An honest man's the noblest work of God;'
And certes, in fair Virtue's heavenly road,
The cottage leaves the palace far behind;
What is a lordling's pomp? a cumbrous load,
Disguising oft the wretch of human kind,
Studied in arts of Hell, in wickedness refin'd!

O Scotia! my dear, my native soil!
For whom my warmest wish to Heaven is sent!
Long may thy hardy sons of rustic toil
Be blest with health, and peace, and sweet content!
And O! may Heaven their simple lives prevent
From Luxury's contagion, weak and vile!
Then, howe'er crowns and coronets be rent,
A virtuous populace may rise the while,
And stand a wall of fire around their much-lov'd isle.

O Thou! who pour'd the patriotic tide,
That stream'd through Wallace's undaunted heart,
Who dar'd to, nobly, stem tyrannic pride,
Or nobly die, the second glorious part:
(The patriot's God, peculiarly Thou art,
His friend, inspirer, guardian, and reward!)
O never, never Scotia's realm desert;
But still the patriot, and the patriot-bard
In bright succession raise, her ornament and guard!

To a Louse

ON SEEING ONE ON A LADY'S BONNET AT CHURCH

Burns finds sympathy and empathy with the humble louse for seeming to have ideas above its station. This poem has another message though, about how we may not realise how we are viewed by others. The fine lady in her expensive bonnet may think she is a cut above the rest, but to the louse she is just dinner!

Ha! whare ye gaun, ye crowlin ferlie?
Your impudence protects you sairly,
I canna say but ye strunt rarely
          Owre gauze and lace,
Though faith! I fear ye dine but sparely
          On sic a place.

Ye ugly, creepin, blastit wonner,
Detested, shunn'd by saunt an' sinner,
How daur ye set your fit upon her—
          Sae fine a lady!
Gae somewhere else and seek your dinner
          On some poor body.

Swith! in some beggar's haffet squattle:
There ye may creep, and sprawl, and sprattle,
Wi' ither kindred, jumping cattle,
          In shoals and nations;
Whare horn nor bane ne'er daur unsettle
          Your thick plantations.

Now haud you there! ye're out o' sight,

Below the fatt'rils, snug an' tight;
Na faith ye yet! ye'll no be right,
               Till ye've got on it—
The vera tapmost, tow'ring height
               O' Miss's bonnet.

My sooth! right bauld ye set your nose out,
As plump an' grey as onie grozet:
O for some rank, mercurial rozet,
               Or fell, red smeddum,
I'd gie ye sic a hearty dose o't,
               Wad dress your droddum!

I wad na been surpris'd to spy
You on an auld wife's flainen toy;
Or aiblins some bit duddie boy,
               On's wyliecoat;
But Miss's fine Lunardi! fye!
               How daur ye do't?

O Jenny, dinna toss your head,
An' set your beauties a' abread!
Ye little ken what cursed speed
               The blastie's makin!
Thae winks an' finger-ends, I dread,
               Are notice takin!

O wad some Power the giftie gie us
To see oursels as ithers see us!
It wad frae monie a blunder free us,
               An' foolish notion:
What airs in dress an' gait wad lea'e us,
               An' ev'n devotion!

ADDRESS TO THE UNCO GUID

OR THE RIGIDLY RIGHTEOUS

*This poem is a speech in defence of the ordinary failings of human-
ity to those who see themselves as 'unco guid', who are in fact too
'rigidly righteous' to look with charity on the faults of others.*

> *My Son, these maxims make a rule,*
> *An' lump them ay thegither:*
> *The Rigid Righteous is a fool,*
> *The Rigid Wise anither;*
> *The cleanest corn that e'er was dight*
> *May hae some pyles o' caff in;*
> *So ne'er a fellow-crature slight*
> *For random fits o' daffin.*
>
> SOLOMON (ECCLESIASTES 7:16)

O ye, wha are sae guid yoursel,
    Sae pious and sae holy,
Ye've nought to do but mark and tell
    Your neebours' fauts and folly;
Whase life is like a weel-gaun mill,
    Supplied wi' store o' water;
The heapit happer's ebbing still,
    An' still the clap plays clatter!

Hear me, ye venerable core,
    As counsel for poor mortals
That frequent pass douce Wisdom's door
    For glaikit Folly's portals:

I for their thoughtless, careless sakes
    Would here propone defences—
Their donsie tricks, their black mistakes,
    Their failings and mischances.

Ye see your state wi' theirs compared,
    And shudder at the niffer;
But cast a moment's fair regard,
    What makes the mighty differ?
Discount what scant occasion gave;
    That purity ye pride in;
And (what aft mair than a' the lave)
    Your better art o' hidin.

Think, when your castigated pulse
    Gies now and then a wallop,
What ragings must his veins convulse,
    That still eternal gallop!
Wi' wind and tide fair i' your tail,
    Right on ye scud your sea-way;
But in the teeth o' baith to sail,
    It maks an unco lee-way.

See Social-life and Glee sit down
    All joyous and unthinking,
Till, quite transmugrify'd, they're grown
    Debauchery and Drinking:
O, would they stay to calculate,
    Th' eternal consequences,
Or—your more dreaded hell to state—
    Damnation of expenses!

Ye high, exalted, virtuous dames,
    Tied up in godly laces,
Before ye gie poor Frailty names,
    Suppose a change o' cases:
A dear-lov'd lad, convenience snug,
    A treach'rous inclination—
But, let me whisper i' your lug,
    Ye're aiblins nae temptation.

Then gently scan your brother man,
    Still gentler sister woman;
Though they may gang a kennin wrang,
    To step aside is human:
One point must still be greatly dark,
    The moving *why* they do it;
And just as lamely can ye mark
    How far perhaps they rue it.

Who made the heart, 'tis He alone
    Decidedly can try us:
He knows each chord, its various tone,
    Each spring, its various bias:
Then at the balance let's be mute,
    We never can adjust it;
What's done we partly may compute,
    But know not what's resisted.

Tam o' Shanter

Tam o' Shanter *is Burns' most famous and most admired poem. (For Burns' own summary of the story* see Ellisland and Dumfries, *page 49.) The characters mentioned in the poem are said to be based on people Burns really knew, and it also shows the influence of the tales of witches and fairies that he heard as a child.*

> *Of Brownyis and Bogillis full is this Buke.*
>   GAVIN DOUGLAS

When chapman billies leave the street,
An drouthy neebors neebors meet;
As market days are wearing late,
An' folk begin to tak the gate;
While we sit bousing at the nappy,
An' getting fou and unco happy,
We think na on the lang Scots miles,
The mosses, waters, slaps, and styles,
That lie between us and our hame,
Whare sits our sulky, sullen dame,
Gathering her brows like gathering storm,
Nursing her wrath to keep it warm.

This truth fand honest Tam o' Shanter,
As he frae Ayr ae night did canter:
(Auld Ayr, wham ne'er a town surpasses.
For honest men and bonie lasses.)

O Tam! had'st thou but been sae wise,
As taen thy ain wife Kate's advice!
She tauld thee weel thou was a skellum,
A blethering, blustering, drunken blellum;
That frae November till October,
Ae market day thou was na sober;
That ilka melder wi' the miller,
Thou sat as lang as thou had siller;
That ev'ry naig was ca'd a shoe on,
The smith and thee gat roaring fou on;
That at the Lord's house, even on Sunday,
Thou drank wi' Kirkton Jean till Monday.
She prophesied, that, late or soon,
Thou would be found deep drown'd in Doon,
Or catch'd wi' warlocks in the mirk
By Alloway's auld, haunted kirk.

Ah! gentle dames, it gars me greet,
To think how monie counsels sweet,
How monie lengthen'd, sage advices
The husband frae the wife despises!

But to our tale:—Ae market-night,
Tam had got planted unco right,
Fast by an ingle, bleezing finely,
Wi' reaming swats, that drank divinely;
And at his elbow, Souter Johnny,
His ancient, trusty, drouthy crony:
Tam lo'ed him like a very brither;
They had been fou for weeks thegither.
The night drave on wi' sangs and clatter;
And ay the ale was growing better:
The landlady and Tam grew gracious
Wi' secret favours, sweet and precious:
The Souter tauld his queerest stories;
The landlord's laugh was ready chorus:
The storm without might rair and rustle,
Tam did na mind the storm a whistle.

Care, mad to see a man sae happy,
E'en drown'd himsel amang the nappy.
As bees flee hame wi' lades o' treasure,
The minutes wing'd their way wi' pleasure:
Kings may be blest but Tam was glorious,
O'er a' the ills o' life victorious!

But pleasures are like poppies spread:
You seize the flow'r, its bloom is shed;
Or like the snow falls in the river,

A moment white—then melts for ever;
Or like the Borealis race,
That flit ere you can point their place;
Or like the rainbow's lovely form
Evanishing amid the storm.
Nae man can tether time or tide;
The hour approaches Tam maun ride:
That hour, o'night's black arch the key-stane,
That dreary hour Tam mounts his beast in;
And sic a night he taks the road in,
As ne'er poor sinner was abroad in.

    The wind blew as 'twad blawn its last;
The rattling showers rose on the blast;
The speedy gleams the darkness swallow'd;
Loud, deep, and lang the thunder bellow'd:
That night, a child might understand,
The Deil had business on his hand.

    Weel mounted on his grey meare Meg,
A better never lifted leg,
Tam skelpit on through dub and mire,
Despising wind, and rain, and fire;
Whiles holding fast his guid blue bonnet,
Whiles crooning o'er some auld Scots sonnet,
Whiles glow'ring round wi' prudent cares,
Lest bogles catch him unawares:
Kirk-Alloway was drawing nigh,
Whares ghaists and houlets nightly cry.

    By this time he was cross the ford,
Whare in the snaw the chapman smoor'd;

And past the birks and meikle stane,
Whare drunken Charlie brak's neck-bane;
And through the whins, and by the cairn,
Whare hunters fand the murder'd bairn;
And near the thorn, aboon the well,
Whare Mungo's mither hang'd hersel.
Before him Doon pours all his floods;
The doubling storm roars through the woods;
The lightnings flash from pole to pole;
Near and more near the thunders roll:
When, glimmering through the groaning trees,
Kirk-Alloway seem'd in a bleeze,
Through ilka bore the beams were glancing,
And loud resounding mirth and dancing.

Inspiring, bold John Barleycorn!
What dangers thou canst make us scorn!
Wi' tippenny, we fear nae evil;
Wi' usquabae, we'll face the Devil!
The swats sae ream'd in Tammie's noddle,
Fair play, he car'd na deils a boddle.
But Maggie stood, right sair astonish'd,
Till, by the heel and hand admonish'd,
She ventur'd forward on the light;
And, wow! Tam saw an unco sight!

Warlocks and witches in a dance;
Nae cotillion, brent new frae France,
But hornpipes, jigs, strathspeys and reels,
Put life and mettle in their heels.
A winnock-bunker in the east,

There sat Auld Nick, in shape o' beast;
A touzie tyke, black, grim and large,
To gie them music was his charge;
He screw'd the pipes and gart them skirl,
Till roof and rafters a' did dirl.
Coffins stood round, like open presses,
That shaw'd the dead in their last dresses;
And, by some devilish cantraip sleight,
Each in its cauld hand held a light;
By which heroic Tam was able
To note upon the haly table,
A murderer's banes, in gibbet-airns;
Twa span-lang, wee, unchristen'd bairns;
A theif new-cutted frae a rape—
Wi' his last gasp his gab did gape;
Five tomahawks wi' bluid red-rusted;
Five scymitars wi' murder crusted;

A garter which a babe had strangled;
A knife a father's throat had mangled—
Whom his ain son o' life bereft—
The grey hairs yet stack to the heft;
Wi' mair of horrible and awefu',
Which ev'n to name wad be unlawfu'.
Three Lawyers' tongues, turned inside out,
Wi' lies seamed life a beggar's clout;
Three Priests' hearts, rotten, black as muck,
Lay stinking, vile, in every neuk.

As Tammie glowr'd, amaz'd and curious,
The mirth and fun grew fast and furious;
The piper loud and louder blew,
The dancers quick and quicker flew,
They reel'd, they set, they cross'd, they cleekit,
Till ilka carlin swat and reekit,
And coost her duddies to the wark,
And linket at it in her sark!

Now Tam, O Tam! had thae been queans,
A' plump and strapping in their teens!
Their sarks, instead o' creeshie flannen,
Been snaw-white seventeen hunder linen!—
Thir breeks o'mine, my only pair,
That ance were plush, o' guid blue hair,
I wad hae gi'en them off my hurdies
For ae blink o' the bonie burdies!

But wither'd beldams, auld and droll,
Rigwoodie hags wad spean a foal,
Louping and flinging on a crummock,
I wonder did na turn thy stomach!

But Tam kend what was what fu' brawlie:
There was ae winsome wench and wawlie,
That night enlisted in the core,
Lang after kend on Carrick shore:
(For monie a beast to dead she shot,
An' perish'd monie a bonie boat,
And shook baith meikle corn and bear,
And held the country-side in fear.)
Her cutty sark, o' Paisley harn,
That while a lassie she had worn,
In longitude though sorely scanty,
It was her best, and she was vauntie....
Ah! little kend thy reverend grannie,
That sark she coft for her wee Nannie,
Wi' twa pund Scots ('twas a' her riches),
Wad ever grac'd a dance of witches!

But here my Muse her wing maun cour,
Sic flights as far beyond her power:
To sing how Nannie lap and flang
(A souple jade she was and strang);
And how Tam stood like ane bewitch'd,
And thought his very een enrich'd;
Even Satan glowr'd, and fidg'd fu' fain,
And hotch'd and blew wi' might and main;
Till first ae caper, syne anither,
Tam tint his reason a' thegither,
And roars out: 'Weel done, Cutty-sark!'
And in an instant all was dark;
And scarcely had he Maggie rallied,
When out the hellish legion sallied.

As bees bizz out wi' angry fyke,
When plundering herds assail their byke;
As open pussie's mortal foes,
When, pop! she starts before their nose;
As eager runs the market-crowd,
When 'Catch the thief!' resounds aloud:
So Maggie runs, the witches folow,
Wi' monie an eldritch skriech and hollow.

Ah, Tam! Ah, Tam! thou'll get thy fairin!
In hell they'll roast thee like a herrin!

In vain thy Kate awaits thy comin!
Kate soon will be a woefu' woman!
Now, do thy speedy utmost, Meg,
And win the key-stane of the brig;
There, at them thou thy tail may toss,
A running stream they dare na cross!
But ere the key-stane she could make,
The fient a tail she had to shake;
For Nannie, far before the rest,
Hard upon noble Maggie prest,
And flew at Tam wi furious ettle;
But little wist she Maggie's mettle!
Ae spring brought off her master hale,
But left behind her ain grey tail:
The carlin claught her by the rump,
And left poor Maggie scarce a stump.

Now, wha this tale o' truth shall read,
Ilk man and mother's son, take heed:
Whene'er to drink you are inclin'd,
Or cutty sarks run in your mind,
Think! ye may buy the joys o'er dear:
Remember Tam o' Shanter's meare.

The Auld Farmer's New-Year Morning Salutation to his Auld Mare, Maggie

ON GIVING HER THE ACCUSTOMED RIPP OF CORN TO HANSEL IN THE NEW-YEAR

The farmer thanks his horse for the hard work that she has done for him now that she is in her old age, and remembers how his youth and hers are linked.

A Guid New-Year I wish thee, Maggie!
Hae, there's a ripp to thy auld baggie:
Though thou's howe-backit now, an' knaggie,
   I've seen the day
Thou could hae gaen like onie staggie,
    Out-owre the lay.

Though now thou's dowie, stiff, an' crazy,
An' thy auld hide as white's a daisie,
I've seen thee dappl't, sleek an' glaizie,
   A bonie gray:
He should been tight that daur't to raize thee,
    Ance in a day.

Thou ance was i' the foremost rank,
A filly buirdly, steeve, an' swank:
An' set weel down a shapely shank
   As e'er tread yird;
An' could hae flown out-owre a stank
    Like onie bird.

It's now some nine-an'-twenty year
Sin' thou was my guid-father's meere;
He gied me thee, o' tocher clear,
            An' fifty mark;
Though it was sma', 'twas weel-won gear,
            An' thou was stark.

When first I gaed to woo my Jenny,
Ye then was trottin wi' your minnie:
Though ye was trickie, slee, an' funnie,
            Ye ne'er was donsie;
But hamely, tawie, quiet, an' cannie,
            An' unco sonsie.

That day, ye pranc'd wi' muckle pride,
When ye bure hame my bonie bride:
An' sweet an' gracefu' she did ride,
                    Wi' maiden air!
Kyle-Stewart I could bragget wide,
                For sic a pair.

Though now ye dow but hoyte and hobble,
An' wintle like a saumont-coble,
That day, ye was a jinker noble,
                    For heels an' win'!
An' ran them till they a' did wauble,
                Far, far behin'!

When thou an' I were young and skiegh,
An' stable-meals at fairs were driegh,
How thou wad prance, an' snore, an' skriegh,
                    An' tak the road!
Town's bodies ran, an' stood abiegh,
                An' ca't thee mad.

When thou was corn't, an' I was mellow,
We took the road ay like a swallow:
At brooses thou had ne'er a fellow,
                    For pith an' speed;
But ev'ry tail thou pay't them hollow,
                Whare'er thou gaed.

The sma, droop-rumpl't, hunter cattle
Might aiblins waur't thee for a brattle;
But sax Scotch miles thou try't their mettle,
                An' gar't them whaizle:

Nae whip nor spur, but just a wattle
            O' saugh or hazle.

Thou was a noble fittie-lan',
As e'er in tug or tow was drawn!
Aft thee an' I, in aught hours' gaun,
            On guid March-weather,
Hae turn'd sax rood beside our han'
            For days thegither.

Thou never braing't, an' fetch't, an' flisket;
But thy auld tail thou wad hae whisket,
An' spread abreed thy weel-fill'd brisket,
            Wi' pith an' pow'r;
Till sprittie knowes wad rair't an' risket,
            An' slypet owre.

When frosts lay lang, an' snaws were deep,
An' threaten'd labour back to keep,
I gied thy cog a wee bit heap
            Aboon the timmer:
I ken'd my Maggie wad na sleep
            For that, or simmer.

In cart or car thou never reestet;
The steyest brae thou wad hae fac't it;
Thou never lap, an' sten't, an' breastet,
            Then stood to blaw;
But just thy step a wee thing hastet,
            Thou snoov't awa.

My pleugh is now thy bairntime a',
Four gallant brutes as e'er did draw;

Forbye sax mae I've sell't awa,
    That thou hast nurst;
They drew me thretteen pund an' twa.
    The vera warst.

Monie a sair daurg we twa hae wrought,
An' wi' the weary warl' fought!
An' monie an anxious day I thought
    We wad be beat!
Yet here to crazy age we're brought,
    Wi' something yet.

An' think na', my auld trusty servan',
That now perhaps thou's less deservin,
An' thy auld days may end in starvin;
    For my last fow,
A heapet stimpart, I'll reserve ane
    Laid by for you.

We've worn to crazy years thegither;
We'll toyte about wi' ane anither;
Wi' tentie care I'll flit thy tether
    To some hain'd rig,
Whare ye may nobly rax your leather
    Wi' sma' fatigue.

Holy Willie's Prayer

Holy Willie's Prayer is one of Burns' harshest and funniest sat-
ires and while the poet was alive it was published anonymously.
The character of Holy Willie is based on a self-righteous church
elder called William Fisher. Gavin Hamilton, mentioned in the
twelfth verse, was Burns' friend whom Fisher accused of neglecting
his worship and had investigated by the Kirk Session—he was
found to be innocent. Robert Aitken in the fifteenth verse was his
counsel during the investigation.

> *And send the godly in a pet to pray.*
>
> POPE

O Thou, wha in the Heavens does dwell,
Wha, as it pleases best Thysel',
Sends ane to Heaven an' ten to Hell
    A' for Thy glory,
And no for onie guid or ill
    They've done before Thee!

I bless and praise Thy matchless might,
When thousands Thou has left in night,
That I am here before Thy sight,
    For gifts an' grace
A burning and a shining light
    To a' this place.

What was I, or my generation,
That I should get sic exaltation?
I, wha deserv'd most just damnation
    For broken laws

Sax thousand years ere my creation,
        Through Adam's cause!

When frae my mither's womb I fell,
Thou might hae plungèd me in hell
To gnash my gooms, to weep and wail
        In burnin lakes,
Whare damnèd devils roar and yell,
        Chain'd to their stakes.

Yet I am here, a chosen sample,
To show Thy grace is great and ample:
I'm here a pillar o' Thy temple,
        Strong as a rock;
A guide, a buckler, and example
        To a' Thy flock!

O Lord, Thou kens what zeal I bear,
When drinkers drink an' swearers swear,

An' singin' there and dancin' here,
      Wi' great and sma';
For I am keepit by Thy fear,
      Free frae them a'.

But yet, O Lord! confess I must,
At times I'm fash'd wi' fleshly lust;
An' sometimes, too, in warldly trust,
      Vile self gets in;
But Thou remembers we are dust,
      Defil'd wi' sin.

O Lord! yestreen, Thou kens, wi' Meg—
Thy pardon I sincerely beg—
O, may't ne'er be a living plague
      To my dishonour!
An' I'll ne'er lift a lawless leg
      Again upon her.

Besides, I further maun avow—
Wi' Leezie's lass, three times, I trow—
But, Lord, that Friday I was fou,
      When I cam near her;
Or else, Thou kens, Thy servant true
      Wad never steer her.

Maybe Thou lets this fleshly thorn
Buffet Thy servant e'en and morn,
Lest he owre proud and high should turn
      That he's sae gifted:
If sae, Thy han' maun e'en be borne
      Until Thou lift it.

Lord, bless Thy chosen in this place,
For here Thou has a chosen race!
But God confound their stubborn face
          An' blast their name,
Wha bring Thy elders to disgrace
          An' open shame!

Lord, mind Gau'n Hamilton's deserts:
He drinks, an' swears, an' plays at cartes,
Yet has sae monie takin arts
          Wi' great and sma',
Frae God's ain Priest the people's hearts
          He steals awa.

And when we chasten'd him therefore,
Thou kens how he bred sic a splore,
And set the warld in a roar
          O' laughin at us:
Curse Thou his basket and his store,
          Kail an' potatoes!

Lord, hear my earnest cry and pray'r
Against that Presbyt'ry of Ayr!
Thy strong right hand, Lord, mak it bare
          Upo' their heads!
Lord, visit them, an' dinna spare,
          For their misdeeds!

O Lord, my God! that glib-tongu'd Aiken,
My vera heart and flesh are quakin
To think how i sat sweatin, shakin,
          An' pish'd wi' dread,

While he, wi' hingin lip an' snakin,
      Held up his head.

Lord, in Thy day o' vengeance try him!
Lord, visit them wha did employ him!
And pass not in Thy mercy by them,
      Nor hear their pray'r,
Bur for Thy people's sake destroy them,
      An' dinna spare!

But, Lord, remember me and mine
Wi' mercies tempral and divine,
That I for grace an' gear my shine
      Excell'd by nane;
And a' the glory shall be Thine—
      Amen! Amen!

Scots, Wha Hae

Burns wrote this poem in 1793, inspired by the story of Robert Bruce's victory over Edward II at Bannockburn. It is Bruce's imagined address to his army before the battle. Scots, Wha Hae *is a song of freedom for Scotland that was still relevant in Burns' time. The song was written at a time when the French Republic had declared war on Britain. Many Scots were still bitter about the union of the Scottish and English parliaments and opposed the British government. Because of the war, it was a dangerous time to voice views about independence as it could lead to imprisonment.*

> Scots, wha hae wi' Wallace bled,
> Scots, wham Bruce has aften led,
> Welcome to your gory bed
> > Or to victorie!
>
> Now's the day, and now's the hour:
> See the front o' battle lour,
> See approach proud Edward's power—
> > Chains and slaverie!
>
> Wha will be a traitor-knave?
> Wha can fill a coward's grave?
> Wha sae base as be a slave?
> > Let him turn and flee!
>
> Wha for Scotland's King and Law
> Freedom's sword will strongly draw,
> Freeman stand or freeman fa',
> > Let him follow me!

By Oppression's woes and pains,
By your sons in servile chains,
We will drain our dearest veins
                    But they shall be free!

Lay the proud usurpers low!
Tyrants fall in every foe!
Liberty's in every blow!
                    Let us do, or die!

Such a Parcel of Rogues
in a Nation

Burns bitterly regretted the loss of Scotland's independence in the parliamentary union of 1707. The 'parcel of rogues' are the Scottish commisioners who 'sold' Scotland, and in Burns' view, reduced a nation to the status of a region.

> Fareweel to a' our Scottish fame,
>   Fareweel our ancient glory!
> Fareweel ev'n to the Scottish name,
>   Sae famed in martial story!
> Now Sark rins over Solway sands,
>   An' Tweed rins to the ocean,
> To mark where England's province stands—
>   Such a parcel of rogues in a nation!
>
> What force or guile could not subdue
>   Through many warlike ages
> Is wrought now by a coward few
>   For hireling traitors' wages.
> The English steel we could disdain,
>   Secure in valour's station;
> But English gold has been our bane—
>   Such a parcel of rogues in a nation!
>
> O, would, ere I had seen the day
>   That Treason thus could sell us,
> My auld grey head had lien in clay
>   Wi' Bruce and loyal Wallace!

But pith and power, till my last hour
    I'll mak this declaration:—
'We're bought and sold for English gold'—
    Such a parcel of rogues in a nation!

CHARLIE, HE'S MY DARLING

Charlie refers to 'Bonnie Prince Charlie', Charles Edward Stuart.
Burns had sympathy with the Jacobite cause to return a Stuart to
the throne.

'Twas on a Monday morning
   Right early in the year,
That Charlie came to our town—
   The Young Chevalier!

CHORUS
An' Charlie, he's my darling,
   My darling, my darling,
Charlie, he's my darling—
   The Young Chevalier!

As he was walking up the street
   The city for to view,
O, there he spied a bonie lass
   The window looking through!

Sae light's he jimped up the stair,
   And tirl'd at the pin;
And wha sae ready as hersel'
   To let the laddie in!

He set his Jenny on his knee,
   All in his Highland dress;
For brawlie weel he ken'd the way
   To please a bonie lass.

It's up yon heathery mountain
   And down yon scroggy glen,
We daur na gang a–milkin
   For Charlie and his men!

It was a' for our Rightfu' King

This is another Jacobite song, sung by the character of a soldier ex-iled in Ireland for the cause of the Stuarts.

It was a' for our rightfu' king
    We left fair Scotland's strand;
It was a' for our rightfu' king,
    We e'er saw Irish land,
        My dear—
    We e'er saw Irish land.

Now a' is done that men can do,
    And a' is done in vain,
My Love and Native Land fareweel,
    For I maun cross the main,
        My dear—
    For I maun cross the main.

He turn'd him right and round about
    Upon the Irish shore,
And gae his bridle reins a shake,
    With adieu for evermore,
        My dear—
    And adieu for evermore!

The soger frae the wars returns,
    The sailor frae the main,
But I hae parted frae my love
    Never to meet again,
        My dear—
    Never to meet again.

When day is gane, and night is come,
    And a' folk bound to sleep,
I think on him that's far awa
    The lee-lang night, and weep,
            My dear—
    The lee-lang night and weep.

Does Haughty Gaul Invasion Threat

The Dumfries Volunteers were a group formed in 1795 to protect the burgh against an attack from French forces. France had been at war with Britain since 1793. Burns was involved in the group's foundation, and they gave him a military style tribute at his funeral. He wrote this song for them. It is a song that on the surface seems patriotic and in favour of the king—a very different point of view from that expressed in Such a Parcel o' Rogues in a Nation *and* Scots, Wha Hae—*but in the last verse, after seemingly damning 'the mob', he contradictingly says 'We'll ne'er forget the People'.*

Does haughty Gaul invasion threat?
    Then let the loons beware Sir!
There's wooden walls upon our seas
    And volunteers on shore, Sir!
The Nith shall run to Corsincon,
    And Criffel sink in Solway,
Ere we permit a foreign foe
    On British ground to rally!

O, let us not like snarling tykes,
    In wrangling be divided,
Till, slap! come in an unco loun,
    And wi' a rung decide it!
Be Britain still to Britain true,
    Amang ourselves united!

But never but by British hands
   Maun British wrangs be righted!

The kettle o' the Kirk and State
   Perhaps a clout may fail in't;
But Deil a foreign tinker loon
   Shall ever ca' a nail in't!
Our fathers' blude the kettle bought,
   And wha wad dare to spoil it,
By heavens the sacrilegious dog
   Shall fuel be to boil it!

The wretch that would a tyrant own,
   And the wretch, his true-sworn brother,
Who would set the mob above the throne,
   May they be damn'd together!
Who will not sing *God save the King*
   Shall hang as high's the steeple;
But while we sing *God save the King*,
   We'll ne'er forget the People!

Epistle to J. Lapraik

An Old Scottish Bard, April 1, 1785

John Lapraik was a fellow poet who, like Burns, had experience of poverty. The occasion mentioned in this epistle (which is another word for a letter) is a family party, a 'rocking', where Burns heard one of Lapraik's songs being sung.

While briers an' woodbines budding green,
And paitricks scraichin loud at e'en,
An' morning poussie whiddin seen,
      Inspire my Muse,
This freedom, in an unknown frien'
      I pray excuse.

On Fasten-e'en we had a rockin,
To ca' the crack and weave our stockin;
And there was muckle fun and jokin,
      Ye need na doubt;
At length we had a hearty yokin,
      At 'sang about'.

There was ae sang, amang the rest,
Aboon them a' it pleas'd me best,
That some kind husband had addrest
      To some sweet wife:
It thirl'd the heart-strings through the breast,
      A' to the life.

I've scarce heard ought describ'd sae weel,
What gen'rous, manly bosoms feel;

Thought I, 'Can this be Pope or Steele,
                    Or Beattie's wark?'
They tauld me 'twas an odd kind chiel
                    About Muirkirk.

It pat me fidgin-fain to hear't,
An' sae about him there I spier't;
Then a' that kent him round declar'd
                    He had ingine;
That nane excell'd it, few cam near't,
                    It was sae fine:

That, set him to a pint of ale,
An' either douce or merry tale,
Or rhymes an' sangs he'd made himsel,
                    Or witty catches,
'Tween Inverness an' Teviotdale,
                    He had few matches.

Then up I gat, an' swoor an aith,
Though I should pawn my pleugh an' graith,
Or die a cadger pownie's death,
                    At some dyke-back,
A pint an' gill I'd gie them baith,
                    To hear your crack.

But, first an' foremost, I should tell,
Amaist as soon as I could spell,
I to the crambo-jingle fell;
                    Though rude an' rough—
Yet crooning to a bodys' sel,
                    Does weel eneugh.

I am nae poet, in a sense;
But just a rhymer like by chance,
An' hae to learning nae pretence;
                    Yet, what the matter?
Whene'er my Muse does on me glance,
                    I jingle at her.

Your critic-folk may cock their nose,
And say, 'How can you e'er propose,
You wha ken hardly verse frae prose,
                    To mak a sang?'
But, by your leaves, my learned foes,
                    Ye're maybe wrang.

What's a' your jargon o' your Schools,
Your Latin names for horns an' stools?
If honest Nature made you fools,
                    What sairs your grammars?
Ye'd better taen up spades and shools,
                    Or knappin-hammers.

A set o' dull, conceited hashes
Confuse their brains in college-classes,
They gang in stirks, and come out asses,
                    Plain truth to speak;
An' syne they think to climb Parnassus
                    By dint o' Greek!

Gie me ae spark o' Nature's fire,
That's a' the learning I desire;
Then, though I drudge through dub an' mire
                    At pleugh or cart,

My Muse, though hamely in attire,
                May touch the heart.

O for a spunk o' Allan's glee,
Or Fergusson's, the bauld an' slee,
Or bright Lapraik's, my friend to be,
                If I can hit it!
That would be lear eneugh for me,
                If I could get it.

Now, sir, if ye hae friends enow,
Though real friends I b'lieve are few;
Yet, if your catalogue be fu,
                I'se no insist:
But, gif ye want ae friend that's true,
                I'm on your list.

I winna blaw about mysel,
As ill I like my fauts to tell;
But friends, an' folks that wish me well,
                They sometimes roose me;
Though, I maun own, as monie still
                As far abuse me.

There's ae wee faut they whyles lay to me,
I like the lasses—Gude forgie me!
For monie a plack they wheedle frae me
                At dance or fair;
Maybe some ither thing they gie me,
                They weel can spare.

But Mauchline Race or Mauchline Fair,
I should be proud to meet you there:

We'se gie ae night's discharge to care,
                    If we forgather;
And hae a swap o' rhymin-ware
                    Wi' ane anither.

The four-gill chap, we'se gar him clatter,
An' kirsen him wi' reekin water;
Syne we'll sit down an' tak our whitter,
                    To cheer our heart;
An' faith, we'se be acquainted better
                    Before we part.

Awa ye selfish, warly race,
What think that havins, sense, an' grace,
Ev'n love an' friendship should give place
                    To Catch-the-Plack!
I dinna like to see your face,
                    Nor hear your crack.

But ye whom social pleasure charms,
Whose hearts the tide of kindness warms,
Who hold your being on the terms,
                    'Each aid the others,'
Come to my bowl, come to my arms,
                    My friends, my brothers!

But, to conclude my lang epistle,
As my auld pen's worn to the grissle,
Twa lines frae you wad gar me fissle,
                    Who am most fervent,
While I can either sing or whistle,
                    Your friend and servant,
                    Robert Burnes.

Address to a Haggis

The status of haggis as the national dish of Scotland may have much to do with the popularity of this poem. Most famously it is recited along with other poems and speeches at Burns suppers on 25 January. The haggis is carried in as if it is part of a formal procession, and it is dramatically cut open by the person reciting the poem.

Fair fa' your honest, sonsie face,
Great chieftain o' the puddin-race!
Aboon them a' ye tak your place,
        Painch, tripe, or thairm:
Weel are ye wordy of a grace
        As lang's my arm.

The groaning trencher there ye fill,
Your hurdies like a distant hill,
Your pin wad help to mend a mill
        In time o' need,
While through your pores the dews distil
        Like amber bead.

His knife see rustic Labour dight,
An' cut ye up wi' ready sleight,
Trenching your gushing entrails bright,
        Like onie ditch;
And then, O what a glorious sight,
        Warm-reekin, rich!

Then, horn for horn, they stretch an' strive:
Deil tak the hindmost, on they drive,

Till a' their weel-swall'd kytes belyve
        Are bent like drums;
Then auld Guidman, maist like to rive,
        'Bethankit!' hums.

Is there that owre his French *ragout*,
Or *olio* that wad staw a sow,
Or *fricassee* wad mak her spew
        Wi' perfect sconner,
Looks down wi' sneering, scornfu' view
        On sic a dinner?

Poor devil! see him owre his trash,
As feckless as a wither'd rash,
His spindle shank a guid whip-lash,
        His nieve a nit;
Through bluidy flood or field to dash,
        O how unfit!

But mark the Rustic, haggis-fed,
The trembling earth resounds his tread,
Clap in his walie nieve a blade,
          He'll mak it whissle;
An' legs, an' arms, an' heads will sned
          Like taps o' thrissle.

Ye Pow'rs wha mak mankind your care,
And dish them out their bill o' fare,
Auld Scotland wants nae skinking ware,
          That jaups in luggies;
But, if ye wish her gratefu' prayer,
          Gie her a Haggis!

Is there for Honest Poverty (A Man's a Man For a'That)

This song was written in January 1795. Burns felt strongly about injustice and snobbery, and the song expresses his hopes for a future where people are all equal.

Is there for honest poverty
    That hings his head, an' a' that?
The coward-slave, we pass him by—
    We dare be poor for a' that!
For a' that, an' a' that!
    Our toils obscure, an' a' that,
The rank is but the guinea's stamp,
    The man's the gowd for a' that.

What though on hamely fare we dine,
    Wear hoddin grey, an' a' that?
Gie fools their silks, and knaves their wine
    A man's a man for a' that.
For a' that, an' a' that,
    Their tinsel show, an' a' that.
The honest man, though e'er sae poor,
    Is king o' men for a' that.

Ye see yon birkie ca'd 'a lord,'
    Wha struts, an' stares, an' a' that?
Though hundreds worship at his word,
    He's but a coof for a' that.
For a' that, an' a' that,
    His ribband, star, an' a' that,

The man o' independent mind,
    He looks an' laughs at a' that.

A prince can mak a belted knight,
    A marquis, duke, an' a' that!
But an honest man's aboon his might—
    Guid faith, he mauna fa' that!
For a' that, an' a' that,
    Their dignities, an' a' that
The pith o' sense an' pride o' worth
    Are higher rank than a' that.

Then let us pray that come it may—
    (As come it will for a' that)—
That Sense and Worth o'er a' the earth
    Shall bear the gree an' a' that!
For a' that, an' a' that,
    It's comin yet for a' that,
That Man to Man the world o'er
    Shall brithers be for a' that.

Lament of
Mary Queen of Scots

ON THE APPROACH OF SPRING

This is a poem about the imprisonment and imminent execution of Mary Queen of Scots.

Now Nature hangs her mantle green
    On every blooming tree,
And spreads her sheets o' daisies white
    Out o'er the grassy lea;
Now Phœbus cheers the crystal streams,
    And glads the azure skies:
But nought can glad the weary wight
    That fast in durance lies.

Now laverocks wake the merry morn,
    Aloft on dewy wing;
The merle, in his noontide bow'r,
    Makes woodland echoes ring;
The mavis wild wi' monie a note
    Sings drowsy day to rest:
In love and freedom they rejoice,
    Wi' care nor thrall opprest.

Now blooms the lily by the bank,
    The primrose down the brae;
The hawthorn's budding in the glen,
    And milk-white is the slae:

The meanest hind in fair Scotland
    May rove their sweets amang;
But I, the Queen of a' Scotland,
    Maun lie in prison strang.

I was the Queen o' bonie France,
    Where happy I hae been;
Fu' lightly rase I in the morn,
    As blythe lay down at e'en:
And I'm the sov'reign of Scotland,
    And monie a traitor there!
Yet here I lie in foreign bands
    And never-ending care.

But as for thee, thou false woman,
    My sister and my fae,
Grim vengeance yet shall whet a sword
    That through thy soul shall gae!
The weeping blood in woman's breast
    Was never known to thee;
Nor th' balm that draps on wounds of woe
    Frae woman's pitying e'e.

My son! my son! may kinder stars
    Upon thy fortune shine;
And may those pleasures gild thy reign,
    That ne'er wad blink on mine!
God keep thee frae thy mother's faes,
    Or turn their hearts to thee;
And where thou meet'st thy mother's friend,
    Remember him for me!

O! soon, to me, may summer suns
   Nae mair light up the morn!
Nae mair to me the autumn winds
   Wave o'er the yellow corn!
And, in the narrow house of death,
   Let winter round me rave;
And the next flow'rs that deck the spring
   Bloom on my peaceful grave.

A Bard's Epitaph

Burns wrote this epitaph in anticipation of his own eventual death. He gives a warning, seemingly from the grave, to any passing poet who may be blessed with the same talent as himself not to indulge in the follies that Burns predicts will be his own downfall and to exercise self-control.

Is there a whim-inspired fool,
Owre fast for thought, owre hot for rule,
Owre blate to seek, owre proud to snool?—
           Let him draw near;
And owre this grassy heap sing dool,
           And drap a tear.

Is there a Bard of rustic song,
Who, noteless, steals the crowds among,
That weekly this area throng?—
           O, pass not by!
But with a frater-feeling strong,
           Here, heave a sigh.

Is there a man, whose judgment clear
Can others teach the course to steer,
Yet runs, himself, life's mad career
           Wild as the wave?—
Here pause—and, through the starting tear,
           Survey this grave.

The poor inhabitant below
Was quick to learn and wise to know,

And keenly felt the friendly flow
        And softer flame;
But thoughtless follies laid him low,
        And stain'd his name.

Reader, attend! whether thy soul
Soars Fancy's flights beyond the pole,
Or darkling grubs this earthly hole
        In low pursuit;
Know, prudent, cautious, self-control
        Is Wisdom's root.

Man was Made to Mourn

The poet meets with an old man who tells him of the many reasons to mourn the 'miseries of man', such as pride, age, remorse, shame and 'man's inhumanity to man'.

A DIRGE

When chill November's surly blast
   Made fields and forests bare,
One ev'ning, as I wander'd forth
   Along the banks of Ayr,
I spied a man, whose aged step
   Seem'd weary, worn with care,
His face was furrow'd o'er with years,
   And hoary was his hair.

'Young stranger, whither wand'rest thou?'
   Began the rev'rend Sage;
'Does thirst of wealth thy step constrain,
   Or youthful pleasure's rage?
Or haply, prest with cares and woes,
   Too soon thou hast began
To wander forth, with me, to mourn
   The miseries of man.

'The sun that overhangs yon moors,
   Out-spreading far and wide,
Where hundreds labour to support
   A haughty lordling's pride:
I've seen you weary winter-sun

Twice forty times return;
And ev'ry time has added proofs
   That man was made to mourn.

'O man! while in thy early years,
   How prodigal of time!
Mis-spending all thy precious hours,
   Thy glorious, youthful prime!
Alternate follies take the sway,
   Licentious passions burn:
Which tenfold force gives Nature's law,
   That man was made to mourn.

'Look not alone on youthful prime,
   Or manhood's active might;
Man then is useful to his kind,
   Supported is his right:
But see him on the edge of life,
   With cares and sorrows worn;
Then Age and Want—O ill-match'd pair!—
   Show man was made to mourn.

'A few seem favourites of Fate,
   In Pleasure's lap carest;
Yet think not all the rich and great
   Are likewise truly blest:
But, oh! what crowds in ev'ry land,
   All wretched and forlorn,
Through weary life this lesson learn,
   That man was made to mourn.

'Many and sharp the num'rous ills
   Inwoven with our frame!

More pointed still we make ourselves
    Regret, remorse, and shame!
And man, whose heav'n-erected face
    The smiles of love adorn,—
Man's inhumanity to man
    Makes countless thousands mourn!

'See yonder poor, o'erlabour'd wight,
    So abject, mean, and vile,
Who begs a brother of the earth
    To give him leave to toil;
And see his lordly fellow-worm
    The poor petition spurn,
Unmindful, though a weeping wife
    And helpless offspring mourn.

'If I'm design'd yon lordling's slave—
    By Nature's law design'd—
Why was an independent wish
    E'er planted in my mind?
If not, why am I subject to
    His cruelty, or scorn?
Or why has man the will and pow'r
    To make his fellow mourn?

'Yet let not this too much, my son,
    Disturb thy youthful breast:
This partial view of human-kind
    Is surely not the last!
The poor, oppressed, honest man
    Had never, sure, been born,
Had there not been some recompense
    To comfort those that mourn!

'O Death! the poor man's dearest friend,
    The kindest and the best!
Welcome the hour my aged limbs
    Are laid with thee at rest!
The great, the wealthy fear thy blow,
    From pomp and pleasure torn;
But, oh! a blest relief to those
    That weary-laden mourn!'

The Deil's awa wi' th' Exciseman

Burns started to work for the excise in 1788. The Deil's awa wi' th' Exciseman *is a comical and self-deprecating song that acknowledges the unpopularity of excisemen (collectors of tax)—so much so that they might be friends with the devil!*

> The Deil cam' fiddlin' through the town,
>   And danc'd awa wi' th' Exciseman,
> And ilka wife cries:—'Auld Mahoun,
>   I wish you luck o' the prize, man!'

CHORUS

> *The Deil's awa, the Deil's awa,*
>   *The Deil's awa wi' th' Exciseman!*
> *He's danc'd awa, he's danc'd awa,*
>   *He's danc'd awa wi' th' Exciseman!*

> 'We'll mak our maut, and we'll brew our drink,
>   We'll laugh, sing, and rejoice, man,
> And monie braw thanks to the meikle black Deil,
>   That danc'd awa wi' th' Exciseman.

> 'There's threesome reels, there's foursome reels,
>   There's hornpipes and strathspeys, man,
> But the ae best dance e'er cam to the land
>   Was *The Deil's Awa wi' th' Exciseman!*'

THE TARBOLTON LASSES

Burns' flirtations with local women are the subject of this humorous poem, which, although light-hearted, reflects Burns' attitude to the courtship of women quite accurately.

If ye gae up to yon hill-tap,
    Ye'll there see bonie Peggy:
She kens her father is a laird,
    And she forsooth's a leddy.

There's Sophy tight, a lassie bright,
    Besides a handsome fortune:
Wha canna win her in a night
    Has little art in courtin.

Gae down by Faile, and taste the ale,
    And tak a look o' Mysie:
She's dour and din, a deil within,
    But aiblins she may please ye.

If she be shy, her sister try,
    Ye'll maybe fancy Jenny:
If ye'll dispense wi' want o' sense,
    She kens hersel she's bonie.

As ye gae up by yon hillside,
    Speir in for bonie Bessy:
She'll give ye a beck, and bid ye light,
    And handsomely address ye.

There's few sae bonie, nane sae guid
    In a' King George' dominion:
If ye should doubt the truth of this,
    It's Bessy's ain opinion!

HANDSOME NELL
(O, ONCE I LOV'D A BONIE LASS)

Handsome Nell *was the first poem that Burns wrote. He was*
fifteen and the subject of his admiration was fourteen-year-old
Nelly Kilpatrick, the daughter of a blacksmith near Mount
Oliphant. It was written in the autumn of 1773.

> O, once I lov'd a bonie lass,
>   Ay, and I love her still!
> And whilst that virtue warms my breast,
>   I'll love my handsome Nell.
>
> As bonie lasses I hae seen,
>   And monie full as braw,
> But for a modest gracefu' mien
>   The like I never saw.
>
> A bonie lass, I will confess,
>   Is pleasant to the e'e;
> But without some better qualities
>   She's no a lass for me.
>
> But Nelly's looks are blythe and sweet,
>   And, what is best of a',
> Her reputation is complete
>   And fair without a flaw.
>
> She dresses ay sae clean and neat,
>   Both decent and genteel;
> And then there's something in her gait
>   Gars onie dress look weel.

A gaudy dress and gentle air
   May slightly touch the heart;
But it's innocence and modesty
   That polishes the dart.

'Tis this in Nelly pleases me,
   'Tis this enchants my soul;
For absolutely in my breast
   She reigns without controul.

MARY MORISON

The inspiration for this poem is uncertain, but it was probably a girl called Alison Begbie, who rejected a proposal of marriage from Burns.

O Mary, at thy window be!
    It is the wish'd, the trysted hour.
Those smiles and glances let me see,
    That make the miser's treasure poor.
    How blythely wad I bide the stoure,
A weary slave frae sun to sun,
    Could I the rich reward secure—
The lovely Mary Morison!

Yestreen, when to the trembling string
    The dance gaed through the lighted ha',
To thee my fancy took its wing,
    I sat, but neither heard nor saw:
    Though this was fair, and that was braw,
And yon the toast of a' the town,
    I sigh'd and said amang them a',
'Ye are na Mary Morison!'

O Mary, canst thou wreck his peace
    Wha for thy sake wad gladly die?
Or canst thou break that heart of his
    Whase only faut is loving thee?
    If love for love thou wilt na gie,
At least be pity to me shown:
    A thought ungentle canna be
The thought o' Mary Morison.

GREEN GROW THE RASHES, O

Burns' admiration for women is charmingly portrayed in this song. The poet comments that Nature first created man with her 'prentice han', but her more accomplished and 'noblest work' was creating women.

There's nought but care on ev'ry han',
    In every hour that passes, O:
What signifies the life o' man,
    An' 'twere na for the lasses, O?

CHORUS
Green grow the rashes, O;
Green grow the rashes, O;
The sweetest hours that e'er I spend,
Are spent among the lasses, O.

The war'ly race may riches chase,
    An' riches still may fly them, O;
An' though at last they catch them fast,
    Their hearts can ne'er enjoy them, O.

But gie me a cannie hour at e'en,
    My arms about my dearie, O;
An' war'ly cares an' war'ly men
    May a' gae tapsalteerie, O!

For you sae douce, ye sneer at this;
    Ye're nought but senseless asses, O;
The wisest man the warl' e'er saw,
    He dearly lov'd the lasses, O.

Auld Nature swears, the lovely dears
  Her noblest work she classes, O:
Her prentice han' she try'd on man,
  An' then she made the lasses, O.

ADVICE TO THE MAUCHLINE BELLES

This is a poem about the effect of popular novels on the girls of Mauchline (Jean Armour, Burns' future wife, was a Mauchline girl). Rob Mossgiel, the character who is going to take advantage of the romantic notions that these books would give them, is a persona (a fictionalised representation) of Burns himself, indulging in some light-hearted role-playing.

> O, leave novels, ye Mauchline belles—
>   Ye're safer at your spinning-wheel!
> Such witching books are baited hooks
>   For rakish rooks like Rob Mossgiel.
>
> Your fine *Tom Jones* and *Grandisons,*
>   They make your youthful fancies reel;
> They heat your brains, and fire your veins,
>   And then you're prey for Rob Mossgiel.
>
> Beware a tongue that's smoothly hung,
>   A heart that warmly seems to feel!
> That feeling heart but acts a part—
>   'Tis rakish art in Rob Mossgiel.
>
> The frank address, the soft caress
>   Are worse than poisoned darts of steel;
> The frank address and politesse
>   Are all finesse in Rob Mossgiel.

Will ye go to the Indies, my Mary?

In a letter to Mr George Thomson, a music collector and publisher, Burns sent the following song with the comment: 'In my early years when I was thinking of going to the West Indies, I took the following farewell of a dear girl'. The girl in question is Mary Campbell to whom he had just been betrothed.

> Will ye go to the Indies, my Mary,
> 　　And leave auld Scotia's shore?
> Will ye go to the Indies, my Mary,
> 　　Across th' Atlantic's roar?
>
> O, sweet grows the lime and the orange,
> 　　And the apple on the pine;
> But a' the charms o' the Indies
> 　　Can never equal thine.
>
> I hae sworn by the Heavens to my Mary,
> 　　I hae sworn by the Heavens to be true,
> And sae may the Heavens forget me,
> 　　When I forget my vow!
>
> O, plight me your faith, my Mary,
> 　　And plight me your lily-white hand;
> O, plight me your faith, my Mary,
> 　　Before I leave Scotia's strand!
>
> We hae plighted our troth, my Mary,
> 　　In mutual affection to join;
> And curst be the cause that shall part us!
> 　　The hour and the moment o' time!

My Highland Lassie, O

This song is inspired by Burns' betrothal to Mary Campbell, and his plans to emigrate.

Nae gentle dames, though ne'er sae fair,
Shall ever be my Muse's care:
Their titles a' are empty show—
Gie me my Highland lassie, O!

CHORUS

Within the glen sae bushy, O,
Aboon the plain sae rashy, O,
I set me down wi' right guid will
To sing my Highland lassie, O!

O, were yon hills and vallies mine,
Yon palace and yon gardens fine,
The world then the love should know
I bear my Highland lassie, O!

But fickle fortune frowns on me,
And I maun cross the raging sea;
But while my crimson currents flow
I'll love my Highland lassie, O!

Although through foreign climes I range,
I know her heart will never change;
For her bosom burns with honour's glow,
My faithful Highland lassie, O!

For her I'll dare the billows' roar,
For her I'll trace a distant shore,

That Indian wealth may lustre throw
Around my Highland lassie, O!

She has my heart, she has my hand,
My secret troth and honour's band!
'Till the mortal stroke shall lay me low,
I'm thine my highland lassie, O!

CHORUS

Farewell the glen sae bushy, O!
Farewell the plain sae rashy, O!
To other lands I now must go
To sing my highland lassie, O!

THE BONIE LASS OF ALBANIE

The 'bonie lass' in question was Charlotte, daughter of Charles
Edward Stuart (Bonnie Prince Charlie).

My heart is wae, and unco wae,
    To think upon the raging sea,
That roars between her gardens green
    An' the bonie lass of Albanie.

This lovely maid's of noble blood,
    That rulèd Albion's kingdoms three;
But O, alas, for her bonie face!
    They hae wranged the lass of Albanie.

In the rolling tide of spreading Clyde
    There sits an isle of high degree;
And a town of fame whose princely name
    Should grace the lass of Albanie.

But there is a youth, a witless youth,
    That fills the place where she should be;
We'll send him o'er to his native shore,
    And bring our ain sweet Albanie!

Alas the day, and woe the day!
    A false usurper wan the gree,
Who now commands the towers and lands,
    The royal right of Albanie.

We'll daily pray, we'll nightly pray,
    On bended knees most fervently,
That the time may come, with pipe and drum
    We'll welcome hame fair Albanie.

AULD LANG SYNE

Auld Lang Syne is a song which is well known all over the world, and is sung at New Year and times of celebration. Burns adapted and improved upon a very old song which to his knowledge had never been written down before. 'Auld lang syne', like so many Scots phrases, doesn't have an exact English equivalent, but 'old time's sake' is quite similar.

Should auld acquaintance be forgot,
And never brought to mind?
Should auld acquaintance be forgot,
And days o' lang syne?

CHORUS

For auld lang syne, my jo,
For auld lang syne,
We'll tak a cup o' kindness yet,
For auld lang syne.

And surely ye'll be your pint-stowp!
And surely I'll be mine!
And we'll tak a cup o' kindness yet,
For auld lang syne.

We twa hae run about the braes
And pu'd the gowans fine;
But we've wander'd monie a weary foot
Sin' auld lang syne.

We twa hae paidl'd i' the burn,
Frae mornin' sun till dine;

But seas between us braid hae roar'd
    Sin' auld lang syne.

And there's a hand, my trusty fiere!
    And gie's a hand o' thine!
And we'll tak a right guid-willie waught,
    For auld lang syne.

Ae Fond Kiss

Burns wrote this beautiful song for Mrs Agnes (Nancy) McLehose after they met for the last time in December 1791.

Ae fond kiss, and then we sever!
    Ae fareweel, and then for ever!
Deep in heart-wrung tears I'll pledge thee,
    Warring sighs and groans I'll wage thee.

Who shall say that Fortune grieves him,
    While the star of hope she leaves him?
Me, nae cheerfu' twinkle lights me,
    Dark despair around benights me.

I'll ne'er blame my partial fancy,
    Naething could resist my Nancy!
But to see her was to love her,
    Love but her, and love for ever.

Had we never lov'd sae kindly!
    Had we never lov'd sae blindly!
Never met—or never parted—
    We had ne'er been broken-hearted.

Fare-thee-weel, thou first and fairest!
    Fare-thee-weel, thou best and dearest!
Thine be ilka joy and treasure,
    Peace, Enjoyment, Love and Pleasure!

Ae fond kiss, and then we sever!
    Ae farewell, alas, for ever!
Deep in heart-wrung tears I'll pledge thee,
    Warring sighs and groans I'll wage thee.

John Anderson, my Jo

*This is an old woman's love song to her aged 'jo' (sweetheart), cel-
ebrating their life together and anticipating their death, not with
dread but in the knowledge that they will still be together even
when their lives here are over.*

John Anderson, my jo, John,
    When we were first acquent,
Your locks were like the raven,
    Your bonie brow was brent;

But now your brow is beld, John,
    Your locks are like the snaw,
But blessings on your frosty pow,
    John Anderson, my jo!

John Anderson, my jo, John,
    We clamb the hill thegither,
And monie a canty day, John,
    We've had wi' ane anither;

Now we maun totter down, John,
    And hand in hand we'll go,
And sleep thegither at the foot,
    John Anderson, my jo!

A Red, Red Rose

Some critics have suggested that this song was not wholly composed by Burns but was drawn, at least in part, from an older Scots song. Nevertheless, it is one of the songs most famously associated with Burns and one of the most beautiful.

O, my luve's like a red, red rose,
    That's newly sprung in June;
O, my luve's like the melodie,
    That's sweetly play'd in tune.

As fair art thou, my bonie lass,
    So deep in luve am I,
And I will luve thee still, my Dear,
    Till a' the seas gang dry.

Till a' the seas gang dry, my Dear,
    And the rocks melt wi' the sun!
O I will luve thee still, my Dear,
    While the sands o' life shall run.

And fare thee weel, my only Luve,
    And fare thee weel a while!
And I will come again, my Luve,
    Though it were ten thousand mile!

HIGHLAND MARY

'Highland Mary' was Mary Campbell, the subject of the poems Will ye go to the Indies, my Mary *and* My Highland Lassie, O *to whom Burns had once been betrothed. They had intended to emigrate to Jamaica together but Mary died, and this poem is a touching depiction of Burns' grief.*

Ye banks and braes and streams around
    The castle o' Montgomery,
Green be your woods, and fair your flowers,
    Your waters never drumlie!
There Summer first unfauld her robes,
    And there the langest tarry!
For there I took the last fareweel
    O' my sweet Highland Mary!

How sweetly bloom'd the gay, green birk,
    How rich the hawthorn's blossom,
As underneath their fragrant shade
    I clasped her to my bosom!
The golden hours on angel wings
    Flew o'er me and my dearie:
For dear to me as light and life
    Was my sweet Highland Mary.

Wi' monie a vow and lock'd embrace
    Our parting was fu' tender;
And, pledging aft to meet again,
    We tore oursels asunder.

But O, fell Death's untimely frost,
  That nipt my flower sae early!
Now green's the sod, and cauld's the clay,
  That wraps my Highland Mary!

O, pale, pale now those rosy lips
  I aft hae kissed sae fondly;
And closed for ay the sparkling glance
  That dwalt on me sae kindly;
And mouldering now in silent dust
  That heart that lo'ed me dearly!
But still within my bosom's core
  Shall live my Highland Mary

AFTON WATER

This is another song of mourning for Mary Campbell.

Flow gently, sweet Afton, among thy green braes!
Flow gently, I'll sing thee a song in thy praise!
My Mary's asleep by thy murmuring stream—
Flow gently, sweet Afton, disturb not her dream!

Thou stock dove whose echo resounds through the glen,
Ye wild whistling blackbirds in yon thorny den,
Thou green-crested lapwing, thy screaming forbear,
I charge you, disturb not my slumbering fair!

How lofty, sweet Afton, thy neighbouring hills,
Far mark'd with the courses of clear, winding rills!
There daily I wander, as noon rises high,
My flocks and my Mary's sweet cot in my eye.

How pleasant thy banks and green vallies below,
Where wild in the woodlands the primroses blow;
There oft, as mild ev'ning weeps over the lea.
The sweet-scented birk shades my Mary and me.

Thy crystal stream, Afton, how lovely it glides,
And winds by the cot where my Mary resides!
How wanton thy waters her snowy feet lave,
As, gathering sweet flowerets, she stems thy clear wave!

Flow gently, sweet Afton, among thy green braes!
Flow gently, sweet river, the theme of my lays!
My Mary's asleep by thy murmuring stream,
Flow gently, sweet Afton, disturb not her dream!

Comin Through the Rye

A light-hearted song about secret romantic meetings and how they are of no one else's business.

Comin through the rye, poor
body,
Comin through the rye,
She draigl't a' her petticoatie,
Comin through the rye!

CHORUS
O Jenny's a' weet, poor body,
Jenny's seldom dry:
She draigl't a' her petticoatie,
Comin through the rye!

Gin a body meet a body
Comin through the rye,
Gin a body kiss a body,
Need a body cry?

Gin a body meet a body
Comin through the glen,
Gin a body kiss a body,
Need the warld ken?

Gin a body meet a body
Comin through the grain;
Gin a body kiss a body,
The thing's a body's ain.

I Love My Jean

The Jean mentioned in the poem is Jean Armour, Burns' wife and it is said to have been composed on their honeymoon.

Of a' the airts the wind can blaw
   I dearly like the west,
For there the bonie lassie lives,
   The lassie I lo'e best.
There wild woods grow, and rivers row,
   And monie a hill between,
But day and night my fancy's flight
   Is ever wi' my Jean.

I see her in the dewy flowers—
   I see her sweet and fair.
I hear her in the tunefu' birds—
   I hear her charm the air.
There's not a bonie flower that springs
   By fountain, shaw, or green,
There's not a bonie bird that sings,
   But minds me o' my Jean.

Ay Waukin', O

The character that the poet adopts in this song is that of a woman who is incapable of sleep because she is grieving for her lost love.

Simmer's a pleasant time:
　　Flowers of every colour,
The water rins owre the heugh,
　　And I long for my true lover.

CHORUS

Ay waukin', O,
　　Waukin' still and weary:
Sleep I can get nane
　　For thinking on my dearie.

When I sleep I dream,
　　When I wauk I'm eerie,
Sleep I can get nane
　　For thinking on my dearie.

Lanely night comes on,
　　A' the lave are sleepin',
I think on my bonie lad,
　　And I bleer my een wi' greetin'.

My Father Was a Farmer

*In this song, despite the poverty and misfortune the poet has suf-
fered, he thinks of the lessons that he was taught by his father—to
behave with decency and honesty—and swears never to be melancholy over such a thing as lack of money.*

My father was a farmer upon the Carrick border, O,
And carefully he bred me in decency and order, O.
He bade me act a manly part, though I had ne'er a far-
　　thing, O,
For without an honest, manly heart no man was worth
　　regarding, O.

Then out into the world my course I did determine, O:
Though to be rich was not my wish, yet to be great was
　　charming, O.
My talents they were not the worst, nor yet my educa-
　　tion, O—
Resolv'd was I at least to try to mend my situation, O.

In many a way and vain essay I courted Fortune's fa-
　　vour, O:
Some cause unseen still stept between to frustrate each
　　endeavour, O.
Sometimes by foes I was o'erpower'd, sometimes by
　　friends forsaken, O.
And when my hope was at the top, I still was worst mis-
　　taken, O.

Then sore harass'd, and tir'd at last with Fortune's vain
　　delusion, O,

I dropt my schemes like idle dreams, and came to this
    conclusion, O:—
The past was bad, and the future hid; its good or ill un-
    tried, O,
But the present hour was in my pow'r, and so I would
    enjoy it, O.

No help, nor hope, nor view had I, nor person to be-
    friend me, O;
So I must toil, and sweat, and broil, and labour to sus-
    tain me, O!
To plough and sow, to reap and mow, my father bred
    me early, O:
For one, he said, to labour bred was a match for For-
    tune fairly, O.

Thus all obscure, unknown, and poor, through life I'm
    doom'd to wander, O,
Till down my weary bones I lay in everlasting slumber,
    O.
No view nor care, but shun whate'er might breed me
    pain or sorrow, O.
I live today as well's I may, regardless of tomorrow, O!

But, cheerful still, I am as well as a monarch in a palace,
    O,
Though Fortunes's frown still hunts me down, with all
    her wonted malice, O:
I make indeed my daily bread, but ne'er can make it far-
    ther, O.
But, as daily bread is all I need, I do not much regard
    her, O.

When sometimes by my labour I earn a little money, O,
Some unforseen misfortune comes gen'rally upon me,
   O:
Mischance, mistake, or by neglect, or my good-natur'd
   folly, O—
But, come what will, I've sworn it still, I'll ne'er be
   melancholy, O.

All you who follow wealth and power with unremitting
   ardour, O,
The more in this you look for bliss, you leave your view
   the farther, O.
Had you the wealth Potosi boasts, or nations to adore
   you, O,
A cheerful, honest-hearted clown I will prefer before
   you, O!

WINTER

The poet associates and compares his own misery with the inevitable bitterly cold weather that accompanies winter. He asks God to help him to endure his problems without question because, like the weather, they are God's will. It was written, probably at Irvine in 1781, when Burns was in a very dark mood.

A DIRGE

The wintry west extends his blast,
  And hail and rain does blaw;
Or the stormy north sends driving forth
  The blinding sleet and snaw:
Wild-tumbling brown, the burn comes down,
  And roars frae bank to brae:
While bird and beast in covert rest,
  And pass the heartless day.

'The sweeping blast, the sky o'ercast,'
  The joyless winter day
Let others fear, to me more dear
  Than all the pride of May:
The tempest's howl, it soothes my soul,
  My griefs it seems to join;
The leafless trees my fancy please,
  Their fate resembles mine!

Thou Pow'r Supreme, whose mighty scheme
  These woes of mine fulfil,
Here, firm I rest, they must be best,

Because they are Thy will!
Then all I want (O, do Thou grant
   This one request of mine!):
Since to enjoy Thou dost deny,
   Assist me to resign.

Ca' the Yowes to the Knowes

This is the earlier of two versions of this song. This version appeared in James Johnson's anthology The Scots Musical Museum. *The second version he remodelled for George Thomson, the music publisher. In this case it is a simple romantic dialogue between a girl and her shepherd lover.*

As I gaed down the water-side,
There I met my shepherd lad:
He row'd me sweetly in his plaid,
   And he ca'd me his dearie.

Chorus

Ca' the yowes to the knowes,
Ca' them them whare the heather grows,
Ca' them whare the burnie rowes,
   My bonie dearie!

'Will ye gang down the water-side,
And see the waves sae sweetly glide
Beneath the hazels spreading wide,
   The moon it shines fu' clearly?'

'I was bred up in nae sic school,
My shepherd lad, to play the fool,
An' a' the day to sit in dool,
   An' naebody to see me.'

'Ye sall get gowns and ribbons meet,
Cauf-leather shoon upon your feet,
And in my arms ye'se lie and sleep,
   An' ye sall be my dearie.'

'If ye'll but stand to what you've said,
I'se gang with you, my shepherd lad,
And ye may row me in your plaid,
   And I sall be your dearie.'

'While waters wimple to the sea,
While day blinks in the lift sae hie,
Till clae-cauld death sall blin' my e'e,
   Ye sall be my dearie.'

KILLIECRANKIE

The Pass of Killiecrankie was the location for a crucial battle of the first Jacobite rebellion on 27 July 1689. The 'Dundee' mentioned in the second verse is Viscount Dundee, John Graham of Claverhouse (he is also called 'Clavers' in the last verse). With 2500 Jacobite highlanders, he attempted to prevent General Hugh Mackay, whose allegiance was with William of Orange, from re-covering Blair Castle and re-establishing a fort at Inverlochy (Fort William). Dundee led the charge but was killed. The Jacobites defeated the royal force but there were many casualties on both sides.

'Whare hae ye been sae braw, lad?
    Whare hae ye been sae brankie, O?
Whare hae ye been sae braw, lad?
    Cam ye by Killiecrankie, O?'

CHORUS

*An ye had been whare I hae been,
    Ye wad nae been sae cantie, O!
An ye had seen what I hae seen
    On the braes o' Killiekrankie, O!*

'I faught at land, I faught at sea,
    At hame I faught my auntie, O;
But I met the Devil and Dundee
    On the braes o' Killiekrankie, O.

'The bauld Pitcur fell in a furr,
    An' Clavers gat a clankie, O,
Or I had fed an Athole gled
    On the braes o' Killiekrankie, O!'

The Birks of Aberfeldie

A song celebrating the beauty of nature: with such gifts any personal misfortune is made to seem less important. Burns is said to have composed this while standing under the falls of Aberfeldy.

Now simmer blinks on flow'ry braes,
And o'er the crystal streamlets plays,
Come let us spend the lightsome days
  In the birks of Aberfeldie!

CHORUS

Bonie lassie, will ye go,
Will ye go, will ye go?
Bonie lassie, will ye go
  To the birks of Aberfeldie?

The little birdies blythely sing,
While o'er their heads the hazels hing,
Or lightly flit on wanton wing
  In the birks of Aberfeldie.

The braes ascend like lofty wa's,
The foaming stream, deep-roaring, fa's
O'er hung with fragrant-spreading shaws,
  The birks of Aberfeldie.

The hoary cliffs are crown'd wi' flowers,
White o'er the linns the burnie pours,
And, rising, weets wi' misty showers
  The birks of Aberfeldie.

Let fortune's gifts at random flee,
They ne'er shall draw a wish frae me,
Supremely blest wi' love and thee
    In the birks of Aberfeldie.

THE BANKS O' DOON

This is the song of a woman, abandoned by her 'fause' love, who is made all the more miserable by the wildlife around her, which is seemingly carefree and happy. She compares their love to a rose that is cruelly stolen from her, leaving her only with its thorn.

Ye banks and braes o' bonie Doon,
    How can ye bloom sae fresh and fair?
How can ye chant, ye little birds,
    And I sae weary fu' o' care!
Thou'll break my heart, thou warbling bird,
    That wantons through the flowering thorn!
Thou minds me o' departed joys,
    Departed never to return.

Aft hae I rov'd by bonie Doon
    To see the rose and woodbine twine,
And ilka bird sang o' its luve,
    And fondly sae did I o' mine.
Wi' lightsome heart I pu'd a rose,
    Fu' sweet upon its thorny tree!
And my fause luver staw my rose—
    But ah! he left the thorn wi me.

O, Whistle an' I'll Come to Ye My Lad

This song tells the story of two people who must act as if they have no interest in one another because it is forbidden, when all the while they are sneaking glances and having secret meetings.

But warily tent when ye come to court me,
And come nae unless the back-yett be a-jee;
Syne up the back-style, and let naebody see,
And come as ye were na comin to me,
And come as ye were na comin to me!

CHORUS

O, whistle an' I'll come to ye, my lad!
O, whistle an' I'll come to ye, my lad!
Though father an' mother an' a' should gae mad,
O, whistle an' I'll come to ye, my lad!

At kirk, or at market, whene'er ye meet me,
Gang by me as though that ye car'd na a flie;
But steal me a blink o' your bonie black e'e,
Yet look as ye were na lookin to me,
Yet look as ye were na lookin to me!

Ay vow and protest that ye care na for me,
And whyles ye may lightly my beauty a wee;
But court na anither though jokin ye be,
For fear that she wyle your fancy frae me,
For fear that she wyle your fancy frae me!

O, Wert Thou in the Cauld Blast

This song was written in 1796 when Burns was having great financial difficulties and was very ill. The song was inspired by hearing Jessy Lewars, who was employed to help the family at this time, playing the piano—some light relief in their troubled household. The poet offered to write verses to any tune that Jessy would play. She chose the tune of an old song called 'The Wren'. The song is now generally sung to music written by Mendelssohn.

O, wert thou in the cauld blast
    On yonder lea, on yonder lea,
My plaidie to the angry airt,
    I'd shelter thee, I'd shelter thee.
Or did Misfortune's bitter storms
    Around thee blaw, around thee blaw,
Thy bield should be my bosom,
    To share it a', to share it a'.

Or were I in the wildest waste,
    Sae black and bare, sae black and bare,
The desert were a Paradise,
    If thou wert there, if thou wert there.
Or were I monarch of the globe,
    Wi' thee to reign, wi' thee to reign,
The brightest jewel in my crown
    Wad be my queen, wad be my queen.

Glossary

THE *ch* and *gh* always have the guttural sound (a sound that is made in the back of the throat). The sound of the English diphthong *oo* is commonly spelled *ou*. A diphthong is a vowel sound that involves the tongue moving in a continuous motion from one position to another. The French *u*, a sound that often occurs in the Scots language, is marked *oo* or *ui*. The *a* in genuine Scots words, except when forming a diphthong or followed by an *e* mute after a single consonant, sounds generally like the broad English *a* in wall. The Scots diphthong *oe*, always, and *ea*, very often, sound like the French *e* masculine. The Scottish diphthong *ey* sounds like the Latin *ei*.

a': *all*
albeit: *although*
abeigh: *at a distance*
aboon: *above*
abread: *abroad, in sight*
abreed: *in breadth*
acquent: *acquainted*
acqueesh: *between*

a'day: *day-long*
adle: *putrid water*
ado: *to-do*
ae: *one*
aff: *off*
aff-loof: *off-hand*
afiel: *afield*
afore: *before*

aft: *oft*
aften: *often*
agee: *on one side*
agley: *askew, wrong*
ahin: *behind*
aiblins: *perhaps*
aik: *oak*
aiker: *acre*
ail: *ill*
ain: *own*
air: *early*
airles: *money*
airn: *iron, a tool of that metal*
airt: *direction*
aith: *oath*
aits: *oats*
aiver: *old horse*
aizle: *hot cinder*
akwart: *awkward*
alake: *alas*
alane: *alone*
alang: *along*
amaist: *almost*
amang: *among*
ambrie: *cupboard*
an: *if*
an': *and*
ance: *once*
ane: *one*
aneath: *beneath*
anent: *concerning*

anes: *ones*
aneugh, aneuch: *enough*
anither: *another*
a's: *all is*
ase: *ash*
asklent: *squint*
aspar: *spread out*
asteer: *stirring*
atains: *at once*
athart: *athwart*
athole: *hawk*
at tour: *moreover*
atweel: *of course*
atween: *between*
aught: *possession*
aughteen: *eighteen*
aughtlins: *in any way*
auld: *old*
Auld Reekie: *Edinburgh (old and smoky)*
auld-warld: *old-world*
aumous: *alms*
aumous-dish: *begging bowl*
ava: *at all*
awa: *away*
awald: *doubled up*
awauk: *awake*
awe: *owe*
awfu': *awful*
awnie: *bearded*
awsome: *frightful*

ayont: *beyond*

ay: *always*

ba': *ball*

babie: *baby*

babie clouts: *baby clothes*

backet: *bucket*

backit: *backwards*

backlins-coming: *coming back*

bade: *asked*

baggie: *belly*

baig'nets: *bayonets*

baillie: *magistrate*

bainie: *bony*

bairn: *child*

baith: *both*

bakes: *biscuits*

ballats: *ballads*

bamboozle: *trick*

ban: *curse*

ban': *bond*

bane: *bone*

bang: *effort*

bannet: *bonnet*

bannock: *thick cake*

barket: *barked*

barley-bree: *whisky*

barm: *yeast*

Bartie: *Devil*

batts: *colic*

bauchles: *old shoes*

bauckie-bird: *bat*

baudrons: *cat*

bauk: *rafter*

bauld: *bold*

bawbee: *halfpenny*

bawk: *untilled ridge*

baws'nt: *white*

bawtie: *dog*

bear: *barley*

bearded-bere: *ripe barley*

beas': *vermin*

beastie: *beast*

bedeen: *immediately*

beet: *fan*

beets: *boots*

befa': *befall*

beft: *beaten*

begrutten: *in tears*

beik: *bask*

belang: *belong*

beld: *bald*

bellum: *assault*

bellys: *bellows*

belyve: *by-and-by*

ben: *into, within*

benison: *blessing*

bent: *field*

bere: *barley*

bestead: *provided*

bethankit: *God be thanked; grace after meal*

beuk: *book*

beyont: *beyond*

bicker (n): *wooden dish*

bicker (v): *stagger*

bide: *stay*

bield: *shelter*

bien: *prosperous*

big: *build*

biggin: *cottage*

biggit: *built*

bill: *bull*

billie: *friend*

bing: *heap*

birk: *birch*

birken-shaw: *small wood*

birkie: *fellow*

birl: *carouse*

birnie: *rough*

birr: *energy*

birses: *bristles*

bit: *place*

bizz: *bustle*

black-bonnet: *church elder*

blastie: *mischievous*

blate: *bashful*

blather: *bladder*

blathrie: *chatter*

blatter: *rattle*

blaud: *large quantity*

blaw: *blow, exaggerate*

blawart: *bluebell*

bleer my een: *dim my eyes*

bleer't: *red-eyed*

bleeze: *flame*

blellum: *babbler*

blether: *chatter*

blin': *blind*

blink: *glance*

blinkers: *spies*

blue-boram: *pox*

blue-gown: *a licensed beggar*

bluid: *blood*

bluntie: *idiot*

blypes: *shreds*

blythe: *cheerful*

boal: *wall cupboard*

bobbit: *curtsy*

bocked: *vomited*

boddle: *farthing*

body: *person*

bogles: *hobgoblins*

bon(n)ie: *beautiful*

boord: *board*

boost: *behoved*

bore: *crevice*

boss: *empty*

bourd: *jest*

bow-hought: *bow-legged*

bowk: *bulk, body*

bow-kail: *cabbage*

bowse: *drink*

bow't: *bent*

brachens: *ferns*
brae: *hillside, slopes*
braid: *broad*
braid–claith: *broad cloth*
braird: *first sprouting of corn etc.*
braik: *harrow*
braindg't: *reeled*
brainge: *barge*
brak: *break*
brander: *gridiron*
brands: *calves of the legs*
brang: *bought*
brankan: *prancing*
branks: *halter*
brankie: *gaudy, smart*
brash: *illness*
brats: *scraps*
brattle: *scamper*
braw: *handsome*
brawlie: *heartily*
braxie: *dead sheep*
breastie: *dim. of breast*
breastit: *sprang*
brechame: *halter*
breckan: *fern*
bree: *juice, whisky*
breeks: *britches*
brent: *smooth, high*
brent-new: *brand-new*
brig: *bridge*

briss: *press*
brither: *brother*
brock: *badger*
brogue: *trick*
broo: *broth*
brose: *oatmeal dish*
browden: *fond*
brownie: *spirit*
browst: *ale*
brugh: *burgh*
brulzie: *brawl*
brunstane: *brimstone*
brunt: *burned*
brust: *burst*
buff: *thump*
bught: *pen*
bughtin-time: *milking-time*
buirdly: *stoutly*
buller: *bubble*
bumbazed: *confused*
bum-clock: *beetle*
bummin: *humming*
bummle: *useless person*
bung: *fuddled*
bunker: *window-seat*
burdie: *dim. of bird, girl*
bure: *bore*
burn(ie): *stream*
burnewin: *blacksmith*
burr-thrissle: *thistle*
busk: *dress*

buskie: *bushy*
buskit: *dressed*
buss: *bush*
bussle: *bustle*
but an' ben: *kitchen and parlour*
butching: *butchering*
byke: *hive, crowd*

ca': *call, drive*
cadger: *hawker*
caff: *chaff*
calf-ward: *enclosure for calves*
callant: *boy*
caller: *bracing*
callet: *girlfriend*
cangle: *wrangle*
canna: *cannot*
cannie: *cautious, gentle*
cantie: *jolly*
cantraip: *magic spell*
cape-stane: *cope-stone*
careerin': *rushing*
care na: *care not*
cark: *anxious*
carle: *old man*
carline: *old woman*
cartes: *cards*
castock: *cabbage stem*
caudron: *cauldron*
cauf: *calf*
cauk: *chalk*

cauld: *cold*
cavie: *(hen) coop*
causey: *causeway, street*
chafts: *chops*
chancy: *fortunate*
change-house: *ale-house*
chantan: *chanting*
chanters: *bagpipes*
chap (n): *liquid measure*
chap (v): *rap*
chapman: *pedlar*
chaup: *stroke*
cheek-for-chow: *cheek-by-jowl*
chiel: *fellow*
chimla: *fireplace*
chimla-lug: *fireside*
chirm: *sing*
chuck: *dear*
chuffie: *fat-faced*
cit: *citizen*
clachan: *village*
claes: *clothes*
claith: *cloth*
clank(ie): knock
clarty: *dirty*
clash: *chatter*
claught: *seized*
claut: *clean*
claver: *clover*
clavers: *tales*
cleed: *clothe*

cleek: *clutch*
cleekit: *linked arms*
cleuch: *ravine*
clink: *coin*
clinkin: *jerking*
clinkumbell: *bell-ringer*
clinty: *stony*
clips: *shears*
clish-ma-claver: *nonsense*
cloot: *hoof*
clout: *patch*
cluds: *clouds*
coft: *bought*
cog: *wooden cup*
commaun: *command*
coman: *coming*
cood: *cud*
coof: *idiot*
cookit: *hid*
coor: *cover*
cooser: *stallion*
coost: *cast*
corbie: *crow*
core: *crowd*
corn't: *fed with oats*
cotter: *cottage-dweller*
couthie: *loving, pleasant*
cowe: *scare*
cowpit: *stumbled*
crabbit: *fretful*
crack: *conversation*

craft: *croft*
craig: *rock*
craigie: *throat*
crambo-jingle: *rhymes*
cranks: *creaking*
cranreuch: *hoar-frost*
crap: *crop*
craw: *crow*
creel: *basket, state of confusion*
creeshie: *greasy*
cronie: *friend*
croon: *hum*
crouchie: *hunchbacked*
crouse: *merry*
crowdie: *porridge*
crowl: *crawl*
crummie: *cow*
crummock: *crooked staff*
crump: *crisp*
cry: *tell*
culzie: *flatter*
cuif: *idiot*
cun: *earn*
curch: *kerchief*
curmurring: *commotion*
curn: *parcel*
curple: *buttocks*
cutled: *courted*
cutty: *short*

daez't: *bewildered*

daffin: *merriment*

dail: *plank*

daidlin: *waddling*

daimen–icker: *occasional ear of corn*

dam: *urine*

damn'd haet: *damn all*

dang: *pushed, knocked*

darg: *work*

darklin: *dark*

daud: *pelt*

daunder: *stroll*

daunton: *subdue*

daur: *dare*

daurt: *dared*

daut: *fondle*

dawd: *lump*

dawin: *dawning*

dearthfu': *expensive*

deave: *deafen*

Deil: *Devil*

deleerit: *delirious*

delvin: *digging*

deray: *disorder*

dern: *hidden*

descrive: *describe*

deuk: *duck*

deval: *descend*

diddle: *move quickly*

dight: *wipe*

dink: *trim*

dinmont: *two-year-old sheep*

dinna: *do not*

dint: *affection*

dizzen: *dozen*

docht: *dared*

dochter: *daughter*

doited: *muddled*

donsie: *self-important, restive*

doo: *dove*

dool: *sorrow*

douce: *prudent, grave*

douk: *duck*

doup: *backside*

dour: *sullen*

dow: *can*

dowff: *dismal*

dowie: *dull, sorrowful*

downa: *cannot*

doxy: *lover, suitor*

doylt: *stupid*

doytin: *doddering*

dozen'd: *torpid*

draigl't: *draggled*

drants: *long prayers*

drap: *drop*

draunting: *drawling*

dree: *suffer*

dreeping: *dripping*

dreigh: *tedious*

driddle: *saunter*

droddum: *backside*

droukit: *drenched*
drouth: *thirst*
drucken: *drunken*
drumlie: *muddy*
drummock: *oatmeal and water*
drunt: *bad mood*
dub: *puddle*
duddies: *ragged clothes*
dunt: *blow*
durk: *dirk*
dusht: *pushed by a ram*
dyke: *dry-stone wall*
dynie: *tremble*
dyvor: *bankrupt*

ear': *early*
eard: *earth*
eastlin: *eastern*
e'ebrie: *eyebrow*
e'e: *eye*
een: *eyes*
e'en: *even*
e'enin: *evening*
eerie: *apprehensive*
eke: *also*
eild: *old age*
elbuck: *elbow*
eldritch: *unearthly*
elekit: *elected*
eller: *church elder*
en': *end*

eneugh, enow: *enough*
esthler: *hewn stone*
ettercup: *spider*
ettle: *aim*
even'd: *compared*
evermair: *evermore*
evite: *shun*
expeckit: *expected*
eydent: *diligent*

fa': *befall, obtain, portion*
fab: *trick*
faddom: *fathom*
fae: *foe*
faem: *foam*
faiket: *excused*
fail: *turf*
fain: *fond*
fair-fa': *good luck*
fairin: *reward, present*
fairy: *tiny*
fait: *neat*
fand: *found*
far-aff: *far-off*
farden: *farthing*
farl: *small oatcake*
fash: *trouble*
Fasten-e'en: *Shrove Tuesday*
fatt'rills: *ribbons*
fauld: *fold*
fause: *false*

faut: *fault*
fawsont: *seemly*
feal: *field*
fear't: *frighted*
fecht: *fight*
feck: *majority*
fecket: *waistcoat*
feerie: *sturdy*
feide: *feud*
feil: *many*
fell: *deadly*
felly: *relentless*
ferlie, ferly: *wonder*
fernyer: *last year*
fey: *fated*
fidgin-fain: *restless*
fiel: *comfortable*
fient: *devilish*
fier: *healthy, friend*
findy: *substantial*
fissle: *tingle*
fit: *foot*
flacht: *handful*
flainen: *flannel*
flawgairies: *whimsies*
fleechin: *wheedling*
fleesh: *fleece*
fletherin: *flattering*
fley'd: *frightened*
flichtering: *fluttering*
flinders: *shreds*

flingin-tree: *timber partition between horses in a stable*
fliskit: *fretted*
flit: *move*
fluther: *hurry*
flyte: *scold*
fochten, foughten: *distressed*
fodgel: *plump*
foggage: *coarse grass*
fon: *fond*
Foorsday: *Thursday*
forby(e): *besides*
forenent: *over against*
forfairn: *worn out*
forgather: *meet*
forgie: *forgive*
forjesket: *jaded*
forrit: *forward*
fother: *fodder*
fou, fow, fu': *full, drunk*
foughten: *troubled*
foul-fa'-ye: *ill befall you*
fouth: *plenty*
fow: *bushel*
frae: *from*
frist: *trust*
fud: *backside*
fu-han't: *full-handed*
fur: *a furrow*
fur-ahin: *hindmost ploughing horse*

furm: *form, bench*
fusionless: *spiritless*
fustit: *decayed*
fyke: *fidget*
fyl'd: *soiled*

gab (n): *mouth*
gab (v): *chatter*
ga'd: *galled*
gae: *go*
gadsman: *ploughboy*
gaet: *way*
gan: *begun*
gane: *gone*
gang: *go*
gangrel: *vagrant*
gar: *make*
gash: *respectable*
gat: *got*
gate: *road*
gaud: *went*
gauger: *exciseman*
gaun: *going*
gawky: *awkward*
gawsie: *jolly, buxom*
gear: *possessions*
Geordie: *guinea*
get: *offspring*
ghaist: *ghost*
gie: *give*
gif: *if*

gimmer-pet: *pet ewe*
gilpey: *young woman*
gin: *against, if, should*
girdle: *griddle*
girn: *snarl*
glaikit: *foolish*
glaum'd: *snatched*
gleyde, gled: *common kite*
glint: *peep*
gloaming: *twilight*
glunch: *frown*
gor-cock: *moorcock*
gos: *goshawk*
gowan: *daisy*
gowd: *gold*
gowdie: *head*
gowdspink: *goldfinch*
graff: *grave*
graith: *harness*
grane: *groan*
grannie: *grandmother*
grat: *wept*
gree: *prize, social degree*
greet: *weep*
gree't: *agreed*
grippit: *gripped*
grozet: *gooseberry*
gropsy: *glutton*
grumphie: *pig*
grun: *ground*
gruntle: *snout*

grushie: *growing*
guddle: *mangle*
Gude: *God*
guid: *good*
guidfaither: *father-in-law*
guidmither: *mother-in-law*
guidman: *master of the house*
guidwife: *mistress of the house*
guid–willie waught: *good-will draught; cup of kindness*
gully: *large knife*
gumlie: *muddy*
gumption: *commonsense*
gut–scraper: *fiddler*

ha': *hall*
habber: *stutter*
haddie: *haddock*
haddin: *possession*
hadna: *had not*
hae: *have*
haerst: *harvest*
haet: *have it*
haffet: *side-lock of hair*
ha'–folk: *servants*
hafflins: *halfway*
hag: *moss*
hain: *spare*
hainch: *haunch*
hairum–scairum: *wild*
hald: *holding*

hale: *hearty*
hallan: *mud partition*
Hallow–mass: *All-Saints Day*
haly: *holy*
hame: *home*
hameart: *home-made*
han: *hand*
hand–wal'd: *hand picked*
hankers: *desires*
hansel: *good-luck gift*
hap: *wrap*
happer: *hopper (of a mill)*
happing: *hopping*
hap–step–an'–loup: *hop, step and leap*
harigals: *entrails*
harkit: *listened*
harn: *coarse linen*
hash: *oaf*
hassock: *great amount*
haster: *perplex*
hastow: *hast thou*
haud: *hold*
hauffet: *temple*
haughs: *hollows*
haurl: *drag*
havins: *manners*
hawkie: *white-faced cow*
healsome: *wholesome*
heapit: *heaped*
hee: *call*

heeze: *raise*
heich: *high*
hen–shin'd: *bow-legged*
here awa: *here about*
herryment: *waste*
hersel: *herself*
het: *hot*
heugh: *crag*
highlan: *highland*
hilti–skiltie: *helter-skelter*
himsel: *himself*
hinderlets: *hind parts*
hindmost: *last*
hing: *hang*
hirplin: *limping*
hizzie: *hussy*
hoast: *cough*
hoddin (n): *coarse cloth*
hoddin (v): *jogging along*
hog–shouther: *jostling with the shoulder*
hool: *the husk*
hoolie: *halt, gently*
Hornie: *Devil*
host: *cough*
hotch: *jerk*
houlet: *owl*
housal: *household*
hov'd: *swollen*
howdie: *midwife*
howe: *hollow, glen*

howk: *dig*
hoy't: *urged*
hoyse: *hoist*
hunder: *hundred*
hunkers: *haunches*
hurchin: *urchin*
hurchyall'd: *tottered*
hurdies: *buttocks*
hure: *whore*
hurl: *crash*

i': *in*
icker: *ear of corn*
idleset: *idleness*
ier–oe: *a great-grandchild*
ilk: *each*
ilka: *every*
ill-deedy: *mischievous*
ill-far'd: *ill-favoured*
Ill-Thief: *Devil*
ill-willy: *ill-natured*
ingine: *genius*
ingle: *fireplace*
ingle-gleede: *blazing fireside*
ingle-lowe: *light from the fire*
inlying: *child-bearing*
inowr: *in and over, close to*
intill: *into*
inwith: *inwards*
I'se: *I shall*
ither: *other*

itsel': *itself*
izles: *embers*

jad: *old horse*
jag: *pin-prick*
jauk: *dally*
jauner: *to talk idly*
jaup: *splash*
jaw: *insolent talk*
jawpish: *tricky*
jeeg: *jerk*
jillet: *jilt*
jinglan: *jingling*
jink: *dodge*
jo: *sweetheart*
jockey-coat: *greatcoat*
jocteleg: *clasp knife*
Johnie Ged's hole: *the grave*
jouk: *dodge*
jow: *swing*
jumpit: *jumped*

kae: *jackdaw*
kail: *cabbage*
kail-runt: *cabbage-stalk*
kail-whittle: *cabbage knife*
kail-yard: *cabbage-patch*
kain: *rents in kind*
kame: *comb*
katy-handit: *left-handed*
kebars: *rafters*

kebbuck: *cheese*
keek: *peep*
keekin'-glass: *mirror*
keel: *chalk*
keepit: *kept*
kelpies: *water-spirits*
ken: *know*
ken't: *knew*
kenspeckle: *easily recognized*
ket: *fleece*
kiaugh: *anxiety*
kin': *kind*
kinch: *noose*
king's hood: *a ruminant's second stomach*
kintra: *country*
kirk: *church*
kirn: *harvest supper*
kirsen: *christen*
kiss caups: *pledge friendship*
kist: *chest*
kitchen: *add relish to*
kith: *acquaintance*
kittle (adj): *difficult*
kittle (v): *tickle*
knaggie: *nobbly*
knap: *smart blow*
knappin-hammer: *stone-breaking hammer*
knoited: *knocked*
knowe: *hillock*

knurl: *dwarf*
kye: *cows*
kyte: *belly*

lade: *load*
lady-landers: *ladybird*
laggen: *bottom of a dish*
laigh: *low*
laiglen: *milking pail*
laip: *lap (as a dog)*
lairing: *sinking*
laith: *loath*
lallan: *lowland*
Lammas: *August 1st*
lammie: *lamb*
landlowper: *vagabond*
lane: *lone*
lang: *long*
lang syne: *long ago*
langsum: *tedious*
lantron: *lantern*
laughan: *laughing*
laun: *land*
lave: *remainder, rest*
laverock: *lark*
law: *hill*
lawin: *bill*
lea': *leave*
leal: *loyal*
lear: *learning*
lee-lang: *live long*

leesome: *pleasant*
leeve: *live*
leeze: *bless*
leister: *spear*
len': *lend*
leugh: *laugh*
leuk: *look*
libbet: *gelded*
lightly: *make light of*
limmer: *mistress*
linket: *skipped*
linn: *waterfall*
lint: *flax*
lippen: *trust*
loan: *lane*
loof: *palm*
loon, loun: *rogue,* lad
loot: *allow*
loup, lowp: *leap*
lowe: *flame*
lowse: *loose*
luckie: *old woman*
luesom: *lovely*
lug: *ear*
lugget: *having ears*
luggie: *two-handled drinking cup*
lum: *chimney*
luntin: *smoking*
lume: *loom*
lure: *rather*
luve: *love*

lyart: *grey, withered*
lye: *lie*

mae: *more*
Mahoun: *Devil*
maik: *equal*
mailen: *arable land*
Maily: *Molly*
mair: *more*
maist: *most*
maister: *master*
mak: *make*
mak'sna: *matters not*
mantie: *gown*
mang: *among*
manteel: *mantle*
mantling: *foaming*
mashlum: *mixed grain*
maskin pat: *teapot*
maught: *might*
maukin: *hare*
maun: *must*
mauna: *must not*
maut: *malt*
maw: *mow*
meere, meare: *mare*
meikle: *large*
melder: *meal-grinding*
mell: *mix*
melvie: *to soil with meal*
men': *mend*

mense: *sense, tact*
menseless: *senseless*
menzie: *follower*
merk: *old Scots coin*
mess john: *church minister*
messin: *cur*
middin: *dunghill*
middin-creel: *dung basket*
middlins: *moderately*
milkin'-shiel: *milking parlour*
mim: *meek*
mim-mou'd: *gently spoken*
min': *remember*
mind: *bear in mind*
mindna: *forget*
minnie: *mother*
mirk: *gloomy*
misca': *abuse*
mishanter: *mishap*
mislear'd: *unmannerly*
mislippen: *disappoint*
mismarrow: *mismatch*
mistaen: *mistaken*
misteuk: *mistook*
mith: *might*
mither: *mother*
moch: *moist*
Mononday: *Monday*
monie: *many*
moolin: *crumb*
mools: *dust*

moop: *nibble*
moosty: *mouldy*
mottle: *dusty*
mou': *mouth*
moubit: *mouthful*
moudiwort:*mole*
muckle: *great*
muir: *moor*
mumpit: *stupid*
muslin-kail: *thin broth*
mutchkin: *English pint*
mysel: *myself*

na': *not*
nack: *trick*
naebody: *nobody*
naething: *nothing*
naig: *pony*
naither: *neither*
nane: *none*
nappy: *ale*
nar: *near*
neebor: *neighbour*
needfu': *needfull*
needna: *need not*
negleck: *neglect*
neist: *next*
neth: *below*
neuk: *corner*
new-ca'd: *newly driven*
newlins: *very lately*

nicher: *neigh*
nicht: *night*
nick: *cut*
nicket: *cheated*
niest: *next*
nieve: *fist*
niffer: *exchange*
nit: *nut*
no: *not*
nocht: *nought*
noddle: *brain*
norlan: *northland*
notour: *notorious*
nourice: *nurse*
nowte: *cattle*
nowther: *neither*

o'boot: *gratis*
ocht: *aught*
ochtlins: *in the least*
o'erlay: *smock*
o'erword: *chorus*
onie: *any*
orra: *extra*
o't: *of it*
oughtlins: *in the same degree*
ouk: *week*
ourie: *shivery*
oursel, oursels: *ourselves*
outlers: *cattle not housed*
out-owre: *above*

owre: *over*
owsen: *oxen*
owther: *either*
owthor: *author*
oxter: *armpit*

pack: *intimate*
paction: *agreement*
paidle (n): *puddle*
paidle (v): dawdle
painch: *paunch*
paitrick: *partridge*
pang: *cram*
parishen: *parish*
parritch: *porridge*
pash: *head*
pat: *pot*
pattle: *plough staff*
paughty: *proud*
pawkie: *cunning*
pechan: *stomach*
pechin: *out of breath*
peet-mow: *peat-stack*
peinge: *whine*
peltry: *trash*
penny-fee: *wages*
penny-wheep: *small beer*
pensfu': *conceited*
philibeg: *kilt*
phraise: *flatter*
pickle: *small quantity*

pimpin: *mean, low*
pine: *pain*
pint-stowp: *pint-measure*
pit: *put*
plack: *pennies*
plackless: penniless
plaister: *plaster*
pleugh, plew: *plough*
pliver: *plover*
plouk: *pimple*
poacher-court: *kirk session*
pock: *pocket*
poind: *seized*
pooch: *pouch*
pook: *pluck*
poortith: *poverty*
pou: *pull*
pouk: *poke*
poupit: *pulpit*
pouse: *push*
poussie: *cat, hare*
pouther: *powder*
pow: *head*
pownie: *pony*
pree'd: *tasted*
preen: *pin*
presses: *cupboards*
preeve: *prove*
prent: *print*
prief: *proof*
priggin: *haggling*

proveses: *provosts*
pu': *pull*
pullishee: *pulley*
pultrous: *lecherous*
puir: *pure*
pund: *pound*
pursie: *small purse*
pussie: *hare*
pyke: *pick*
pyle: *grain*
pystle: *epistle*

quaite: *quiet*
quat: *quit*
quauk: *quake*
quey: *cow*
quine: *young woman*
quer: *choir*
quo: *quoth*

rade: *rode*
raff: *plenty*
raffan: *hearty*
ragweed: *ragwort*
raible: *nonsense*
rair: *roar*
ramfeezl'd: *exhausted*
ramgunshoch: *rugged*
rampin': *raging*
ram-stam: *headlong*

randie: *riotous*
rape: *rope*
raploch: *homespun*
rash: *rush*
rattle: *strike*
ratton: *rat*
raucle: *fearless*
raught: *reached*
raw: *row*
rax: *stretch*
ream: *froth*
reave: *rob*
red: *advise*
reek: *smoke*
remead: *remedy*
reuth: *pity*
richt: *right*
rief: *thieve*
rig: *ridge*
riggin: *roof*
rigwoodie: *girdle for a cart horse*
rin: *run*
ringle-ey'd: *white-eyed*
ripp: *handful of corn*
riskit: *cracked*
rither: *rudder*
rive: *split*
roon: *round*
roose: *reputation*
roosty: *rusty*
row(e): *roll, wrap*

rowth: *plenty*
rowtin: *lowing*
royd: *wild*
rozet: *rosin*
rugh: *rough*
rullions: *coarse shoes*
rummle: *stir about*
rummlegumption: *common sense*
rumple: *rump*
run: *downright*
rung: *cudgel*
runkle: *wrinkle*
ruth: *sorrow*
ryke: *reach*

sab: *sob*
sae: *so*
saebins: *since it is so*
saft: *soft*
saikless: *innocent*
sair (v): *serve*
sair (adj): *sore, hard*
sairie: *sorrowful*
sall: *shall*
sark: *shirt*
saul: *soul*
saumont: *salmon*
saunt: *saint*
saut: *salt*
saw: *sow*

sax: *six*
scail: *spill*
scaith: *injury*
scantlins: *scarcely*
scar: *scare*
sconner: *disgust*
scraichin: *screaming*
scrievin: *moving along*
scrimpit: *short*
sculduddery: *fornication*
see'd: *saw*
seelfu: *pleasant*
seenle: *seldom*
session: *court*
set: *start*
shachl't: *distorted*
shanks: *legs*
shanna: *shall not*
shaul: *shallow*
shavie: *prank, trick*
shaw (n): *woodland*
shaw (v): *show*
shawpit: *shelled*
shaws: *stalks*
sheugh: *ditch*
sheuk: *shook*
shiel: *shed*
shool: *shovel*
shoon: *shoes*
shot: *sort*
shouldna: *should not*

shouther: *shoulder*

sic, sik: *such*

sicker: *steady*

sidelins: *sideways*

siller: *silver*

simmer: *summer*

sin: *since*

sirple: *sip*

skaith: *damage*

skeigh: *skittish*

skellum: *rogue*

skelpin: *rushing*

skilly: *skilful*

skinking: *watery*

skinklin: *small*

skirl: *shriek*

sklent: *side-look*

skrimmish: *skirmish*

skurrivaig: *vagabond*

skyre: *shine*

skyte: *lash*

slade: *slid*

slae: *sloe*

slaik: *lick*

slap: *gap*

slaw: *slow*

slee: *sly*

sleekit: *sleek*

sloken: *slake*

sma': *small*

smack: *kiss*

smawly: *small*

smeddum: *powder*

smeek: *smoke*

smiddie, smiddy: *smithy*

smirtle: *bashful smile*

smoor: *smother*

smurr: *drizzle*

smytrie: *litter*

snakin: *sneering*

snash: *abuse*

snaw: *snow*

sned: *cut off*

snell: *sharp*

sneshin: *snuff*

snick: *latch*

snirtle: *snigger*

snool: *snub*

snowkit: *snuffed*

sodger: *soldier*

sole: *sill*

sonnet: *song*

sonsie: *pleasant*

soom: *swim*

soor: *sour*

souk: *suck*

souple: *supple*

souter: *cobbler*

sowp: *spoonful*

sowther: *solder*

spae: *foretell*

spair: *spare*

spak: *spoke*
spean: *wean*
speat: *spate*
speel: *climb*
speet: *skewer*
speir: *ask*
spelder: *tear apart*
spence: *parlour*
spleuchan: *tobacco pouch*
splore: *carousal, disturbance*
sprattle: *scramble*
spreckle: *speckled*
sprittie: *full of spirits*
sprush: *dressed-up*
spunk: *spirit*
spunkie: *will o' the wisp*
squattle: *squat*
stab: *stake*
stacher: *stagger*
stan': *stand*
stane: *stone*
stang: *sting*
stank: *pool*
stap: *stop*
stapple: *stopper*
stark: *strong*
staumrel: *silly*
staw: *sicken; stole*
staw (n): *surfeit*
stechin: *cramming*
steek: *stitch*

steer: *stir*
steeve: *compact*
stell: *still*
stent: *duty*
steyest: *steepest*
stibble: *stubble*
stickit: *stuck*
stimpart: *quarter measure*
stirk: *young cow*
stoiter: *stumbled*
stotter: *stagger*
stoun/stown: *stolen*
stounds: *aches*
stoure: *battle; dust*
stowp: *cup*
strae: *straw*
stak: *stuck*
straik: *stroke*
stramash: *brawl*
strang: *strong*
straught: *straight*
stravaugin: *roaming*
streekit: *stretched*
streen: *last night*
striddle: *straddle*
studdie: *anvil*
stumle: *stumble*
stump: *halt*
stumpie: *stout*
sturt: *fret*
sucker: *sugar*

sugh: *sigh*
sumph: *blockhead*
sune: *soon*
suthron: *southern*
swaird: *sward*
swall'd: *swelled*
swally: *swallow*
swankie: *fine fellow*
swarf: *to swoon*
swat: *sweated*
swatch: *sample*
swats: *light beer*
swee: *over*
sweer: *lazy*
swith: *get away*
swither: *hesitate*
swoor: *swore*
syne: *since, then*

tack: *lease*
tackets: *shoe-nails*
tae: *toe*
taen: *taken*
taigle: *hinder*
taikle: *tackle*
tairge: *target*
taisle: *tassel*
tak: *take*
tald: *told*
tangs: *tongs*
tap: *top*

tapetlesss: *thoughtless*
tapsalteerie: *topsy-turvy*
tassie: *cup*
tauk: *talk*
tauld: *told*
tawted: *matted*
teat: *small quantity*
ted: *spread*
teen: *anger*
tensum: *ten together*
tent (n): *caution*
tent (v): *tend*
tentie: *careful*
teugh: *tough*
teuk: *took*
thack: *thatch*
thae: *those*
thairm: *fiddle-string, intestines*
thankit: *thanked*
thegither: *together*
themsel, themsels: *themselves*
thereanent: *concerning that*
thick: *intimate*
thieveless: *forbidding*
thiggin: *begging*
thir: *these*
thirl: *thrill*
thocht: *thought*
thole: *endure*
thon: *you*
thou'se: *thou shalt*

thowe: *thaw*

thrang (n): *a crowd*

thrang (adj): *busy*

thrapple: *throat*

thrave: *twenty-four sheaves of corn*

thraw: *twist*

threed: *thread*

threep: *maintain*

threesum: *three together*

thretteen: *thirteen*

thretty: *thirsty*

thrist: *thirst*

thrissle: *thistle*

throu'ther: *confused*

thumpit: *thumped*

thurst: *thrust*

thysel: *thyself*

till't: *to it, tilled*

timmer: *timber*

timmer-tuned: *unmusical*

tip/toop: *ram (tup)*

tipper-taiper: *teeter*

tine: *lose*

tinkler: *tinker*

tint: *lost*

tippence: *twopence*

tippenny: *twopenny beer*

tir: *tap*

tither: *other*

tittle: *whisper*

tocher: *marriage bonds*

tod: *fox*

Tod Lowrie: *fox*

too fa': *lean-to*

toom: *empty*

tother: *other*

toun: *farmland*

towsie/tousie: *shaggy*

tow: *rope*

towsing: *handling*

towmond: *twelve-month*

toy: *cap*

tozie: *tipsy*

traiket: *disordered*

trashtrie: *rubbish*

trig: *neat*

trowth: *trust*

tryste: *appointment*

try't: *tried*

tuffle: *ruffle*

tulzie: *quarrel*

tummle: *tumble*

tummler: *cup*

ture: *tore*

turkasses: *pincers*

turn: *task*

turrs: *turfs*

twa, tway: *two*

'twad: *would have*

twahaund: *between two*

twal: *twelve*

twasum: *two together*
twa-three: *some*
tweesh: *betwixt*
twin: *separate from*
twine: *twist*
Tyesday: *Tuesday*
tyke: *dog*
tyken: *bed linen*
tylie: *slice of beef*
tyest: *entice*

ulzie: *oil*
unchancy: *dangerous*
unco: *strange, very*
undeemous: *inconceivable*
undocht: *silly*
uneith: *difficult*
unfauld: *unfold*
unfeiry: *inactive*
unkend: *unknown*
unkin: *unkind*
unloosome: *unlovely*
unsicker: *uncertain*
unsneck: *unlock*
unweeting: *unwittingly*
uphaud: *uphold*
upo': *upon*
upsides: *equal to*
upstan't: *stood*
uptack: *comprehension*
usquebah: *whisky*

vauntie: *proud*
vera, verra: *very*
virl: *ring*
vittles: *food*
vively: *clearly*
vogie: *conceited*
vowt: *vault*

wa': *wall*
wab: *web*
wabster: *weaver*
wad: *wager*
wad: *would*
waddin': *wedding*
wadna: *would not*
wae: *woe*
waeness: *sadness*
waesucks: *alas*
wair'd: *spent*
wale: *choice*
walie: *large*
wame: *belly*
wan: *won*
wanchancie: *dangerous*
wanrestfu': *restless*
wanruly: *unruly*
wanwordy: *unworthy*
wap: *wrap*
wappon: *weapon*
war: *were*
ware: *worn*

wark: *work*

warl'/warld: *world*

warl's gear: *worldly possessions*

warlock-breef: *magic spell*

warl'y: *worldly*

warna: *were not*

warran: *warrant*

warse: *worse*

warsle: *wrestle*

wart: *were it*

wast: *west*

wat: *wet*

water-fit: *river's mouth*

waud: *wade*

waugh: *damp*

waught: *large drink*

wauk: *wake*

waukrife: *sleepless*

waukit: *calloused*

waur: *worse*

wawlie: *handsome*

wean: *child*

weary fa': *plague upon*

weason: *gullet*

wecht: *weight*

weed: *clothes*

weel: *well*

weel-hain'd: *well-saved*

weet: *wet*

westlin: *westerly*

wha: *who*

whae: *who*

whaizle: *wheeze*

whalpit: *whelped*

whang: *slice*

whan: *when*

whar: *where*

whase: *whose*

whaup: *curlew*

wheen: *quantity*

whid: *fib, move quickly, frisk*

whigmaleeries: *whimsical ornaments*

whilk: *which*

whirligigums: *useless things*

whisht: *silence*

whitter: *measure of liquor*

whommilt: *turned upside down*

whun: *basalt*

whunner: *rattle*

whup: *whip*

whyles: *sometimes*

wi': *with*

wifie: *dim. of wife*

willyart: *awkward*

wimple (v): *wind*

wimplin: *winding*

winch: *wench*

winna: *will not*

winnins: *earnings*

winnock-bunker: *window seat*

win's: *winds*
wise-like: *respectable*
wiss: *wish*
witten: *knowledge*
wonner: *wonder*
woo': *wool*
woodie: *gallows*
wook: *weak*
wordy: *worthy*
wrack: *vex*
wraith: *spirit*
wrang: *wrong*
wran: *wren*
wright: *carpenter*
writer: *lawyer*
wud: *wild*
wuddie *rope*
wull: *will*
wure: *wore*
wursum: *putrid matter*
wurtle: *writhe*
wyliecoat: *flannel vest*
wyle: *entice*
wyss: *wise*
wyte: *blame*

yad: *old mare*
yaird: *yard*
yauld: *vigorous*
yaumer: *murmur*
ye: *you*
ye'd: *you would*
ye'll: *you will*
yell: *barren*
yellockin: *squalling*
yer: *your*
yersel: *yourself*
ye'se: *ye shall*
yestreen: *yesternight*
yett: *gate*
yill: *ale*
yince: *once*
yird: *earth*
yirdit: *buried*
yokin: *set to*
yon: *that*
yonner: *yonder*
'yont: *beyond*
younker: *youth*
yowe: *ewe*
yowie: *lamb*

Index of Titles and First Lines